Righteousness *Through* Marriage

Righteousness *Through* Marriage

Marriage in the context of the great controversy

Tapera Chivhaka

EXCELLER BOOKS™
A GLOBAL PRESS

Righteousness through Marriage
Marriage in the context of the great controversy

Cover design by Exceller Books using resources from Pixabay.com

ISBN: 978-81-19524-48-8

First published in India in 2024 by Exceller Books,
An Imprint of GE Group
Address: G1, Dream Apartment, Degree College Road, Belgharia, Kolkata, 700056, India

EXCELLER BOOKS™
A GLOBAL PRESS

www.excellerbooks.com

Acknowledgments

I would like to express my heartfelt gratitude to all those who have seen me through this book, provided support, talked things over with me, read, wrote, offered comments, allowed me to quote their remarks and assisted in the editing, proofreading and designing.

I would like to thank Pastor Michael R. Ngwaru for referring me to Boutique Books, where I received professional help to get this book published.

Above all, I want to thank my wife, Gloria, and the rest of my family, who supported and encouraged me even when I had to stay away from them. It was a long and difficult journey for them.

Last but not least, I apologize to all those whose names I could not mention despite their lifelong support.

Table of Contents

Introduction

Statisticians generally agree that 50% of all marriages end up in divorce. The divorce rate for second and third marriages is about 73%. In marriage, practice does not bring perfection. Of the 50% of couples who are still in their first marriage, less than 10% live a happy, fulfilling married life. There is a simple reason why the statistics are so high: people have looked to the wrong source for marriage solutions. The Bible is the only book that clearly states that marriage was originated by the Creator, God. As such, all matters of marriage should be addressed by the same Bible. People have looked to human rights groups for solutions to marital problems. However, the reality is that these groups will never offer any solution because they are not the originators of marriage in the first place.

The institution of marriage was originated and ordained by God in heaven, and He is the one who offers guidelines on how to start, maintain and live in a marriage. It is just like a car. A car called *Ford* was manufactured by the Ford Company. It gives a manual to anyone who purchases the car so that the car is treated correctly. If the car does not work properly, the user will also refer to the manual to find out how to fix the mechanical problem. In the case of marriage, too, the God of heaven who created marriage has given an instruction manual to all those who want to be married. The instruction manual is called the Bible. Anyone who is serious about the institution of marriage must devote a lot of time to studying this manual. I appreciate that there are a lot of books that have been written about marriage, including this one, but none will substitute for the Bible. The

Bible is the original manual from the Originator of marriage, and it should remain this way.

In the first book of the Bible (Genesis), God, the Creator, introduces us to two institutions that are holy. These institutions are *marriage* and *the Sabbath*. These two institutions were created by God for a purpose. The major purpose is to sanctify people so that they are able to meet the Saviour when He comes on earth to take those who are holy to heaven. Since the purpose of marriage and the Sabbath is to make people holy, the devil has made it his primary purpose to attack these twin institutions. This book will focus on marriage and how God has designed it to overcome the devil. The devil knows that if he destroys the family, the church of God is automatically destroyed, for God's church is nothing but an extension of the family. God's church, to a large extent, reflects the society in which it is located, for the society is a reflection of each family unit that makes it up.

It is unfortunate that humanity has gone out of its way to seek methods of healing marriage in the twenty-first century. There has been an increase in human rights groups such as LGBT rights groups, Child Line, POWA, women empowerment groups and many more. These organizations have been created supposedly to preserve happiness and prevent abuse in the family. However, the reality is that the more the groups are mushrooming, the more the families are suffering.

Incidents witnessed by the people in South Africa give a clear picture of how families are suffering in this age of "enlightenment." People have witnessed how Reeva Steenkamp died at the hands of Oscar Pistorius, Reeva's loved one, on the day the world celebrates as the day of love, Valentine's Day. Due to the wide media coverage of the story, people have witnessed how this murder caused unforgettable pain in many families.

People have seen how wives have been murdered by their husbands for money and how husbands have been murdered by their wives for the same or some other reason. People have witnessed girl children being raped by their fathers and many more incidents. People have been hurt by those who promised to love them the most. In all these incidents, people have witnessed human rights activists clamouring for the blood of the offenders. Unfortunately, this has not seemed to reduce the pain and suffering experienced by people at the hands of those they love most.

It is also sad that the church, which boasts about being founded on *Sola Scriptura* – a phrase that means that the Bible, and the Bible alone, is the sole authority in matters of doctrine and practice – has also borrowed ways of fighting marriage problems from the world. The church has departed from the marriage manual, the Bible and has decided to use ideas from human rights groups to fight abuse, negligence and divorce. Recently, there has been the introduction of the *End it Now* concept, which supposedly will end abuse in families before Jesus comes. The church has even prescribed divorce as one way of getting out of abusive families. As a result, divorce is now being viewed in a different light from what the Bible says. Gay marriages are slowly being accepted in the family. All this is a way of trying to find satisfactory answers to marriage problems.

The world has resorted to marriage perversions, such as homosexual, lesbian, gay, polygamous and living-in "marriages", all in pursuit of happiness and freedom. However, the result has always been the same: abuse, hurt, pain, suffering and ultimately death. There have been rigorous debates in the church about women's ordination, which, in its etymological sense, will empower women to take leadership positions in the church. Woman ordination is a concept that is strange to the Bible. Empowering women will, according to advocates of women empowerment, stop women and children from being abused by monsters called men. But, as I have reiterated again and again, neither women empowerment nor woman ordination nor *End it Now* will end or reduce the incidence of violence in families. The answer to all marriage problems does not lie in human beings because no human being invented marriage. It lies in God.

In the process of trying to justify or explain the two concepts – woman ordination and *End it Now* – the church has gone as far as misquoting or misrepresenting the word of God. It has gone as far as even trying to change the wording of the Bible, for instance, suggesting that where there is the word *he*, it should be replaced by an inclusive word representing both genders. In the process of trying to stop abuse in families, the Bible has suffered abuse in this day and age. However, the results have shown that abusing the Bible will result in increased abuse in families.

In this small book, I will explain why God instituted the marriage ceremony. The functioning of marriage should be placed in God's purpose for it to fulfil its intended purpose on planet Earth. I will follow this thought throughout the book. No amount of human invention will make marriage work because no human being was consulted by God when He instituted marriage.

1| It Is Not Good for a Man to Be Alone

Genesis 1:26 – *And God said, "Let us make man in our image, after our likeness: and let them have dominion over the fish of the sea, and over the fowl of the air, and over the cattle, and over all the earth, and over every creeping thing that creepeth upon the earth."*
1:27 – *So God created man in his own image, in the image of God created he him; male and female created he them.*
1:28 – *And God blessed them, and God said unto them, "Be fruitful, and multiply, and replenish the earth, and subdue it: and have dominion over the fish of the sea, and over the fowl of the air, and over every living thing that moveth upon the earth."*
Genesis 2:15 - *And the LORD God took the man, and put him into the Garden of Eden to dress it and to keep it.*
2:16 – *And the LORD God commanded the man, saying, "Of every tree of the garden thou mayest freely eat:*
2:17 – *But of the tree of the knowledge of good and evil, thou shalt not eat of it: for in the day that thou eatest thereof thou shalt surely die."*
2:18 – *And the LORD God said, "It is not good that the man should be alone; I will make a helper suitable for him."*
2:19 – *And out of the ground the LORD God formed every beast of the field, and every fowl of the air; and brought them unto Adam to see what he would call them: and whatsoever Adam called every living creature, that was the name thereof.*
2:20—*And Adam gave names to all cattle, and to the fowl of the air, and to every beast of the field, but for Adam, there was no helper right for him.*

2:21 – *And the LORD God caused a deep sleep to fall upon Adam, and he slept: and he took one of his ribs, and closed up the flesh instead thereof;*
2:22 – *And the rib, which the LORD God had taken from man, made he a woman, and brought her unto the man.*
2:23 – *And Adam said, "This is now bone of my bones, and flesh of my flesh: she shall be called Woman because she was taken out of Man.*
2:24 – *Therefore shall a man leave his father and his mother, and shall cleave unto his wife: and they shall be one flesh."*
2:25 – *And they were both naked, the man and his wife, and were not ashamed.*
Malachi 2:15 – *And did not he make one? Yet had he the residue of the spirit. And wherefore one? That he might seek a godly seed. Therefore, take heed to your spirit, and let none deal treacherously against the wife of his youth.*

The institution of marriage has its origin in the Bible. There are no other writings on the planet Earth that testify to the fact that marriage came to exist apart from through the God of the Bible.

Genesis chapter 2, quoted above, gives the order in which God created the human family. God created Adam first and gave him duties that he had to perform. God gave Adam the Garden of Eden to keep and care for it. So, work was given to Adam. God also gave the law to Adam. The law concerning the tree of the knowledge of good and evil was given to Adam. Therefore, God crowned Adam with priesthood right from the beginning. Adam was given the role of naming all the beasts of the fields, the birds of the air and the fish of the waters. This all happened in the absence of Eve. After this, God saw that it was not good for a man to be alone. He caused Adam to have a deep sleep and made Eve out of his rib and handed her to Adam. Adam did not suggest to God that he wanted a helper, but God said it was not good for Adam to be alone.

When it comes to marriage, a man does not decide whether to get married or not. God Himself has declared that it is not good for a man to be alone. No amount of civilization, enlightenment or illumination will make it good for a man to be alone. It was not a man who decided that it was not good for him to be alone, and by the same token, there is no man under heaven who can decide that it is good for him to be alone.

Adam did not ask for a wife; God gave her to him. God did not even consult him. That's why Adam was caused to have a deep sleep during the process of creating Eve. Adam had no say. It is imperative for us to bear in mind that it is God who initiated the institution of marriage and finished it without consulting a human being. All Adam did was appreciate the woman who was in front of him after he woke up. The creation of Eve after Adam on the side of God was not an afterthought. It served to fulfil two critical objectives. The first one was to define the roles of Adam and Eve. If Adam had been given his role in the presence of Eve, there was bound to be confusion. Eve would have had a right to claim that some of the roles that God gave to Adam were hers if God had given them to him in her presence. This role distinction is very critical in the marriage, as I will discuss shortly.

The other reason why Eve was created after Adam was that God wanted to create a vacuum in Adam that was not going to be filled by all the animals to whom he was giving names. Though Adam did not know why there was an empty space in his life, God knew why because He had purposely designed it. The Bible clearly states that, as Adam was going on with his duties of tilling the garden and naming the animals, no suitable helper was found for him. The creation of Eve allowed Adam to appreciate his wife, and he never wanted to lose her, as we shall see later. This created a "till death do us part" situation.

When Genesis 1 gives a summary of creation before the details of Genesis 2, it is clear that God intended to create two of them in His image. God never created Adam in His image. There is no single person who can reflect the image of God. A single person can reproduce the character of Jesus in himself or herself but can never reflect the image of God. The image of God is reflected in a marriage, in a couple. The Bible clearly states: "So God created man in his own image, in the image of God created he him; male and female created he them."

The image of God is reflected in the "them," in the "male and female," in the "couple," and in the "marriage." No union, unless it is a marriage between a male and a female, can reflect the image of God. Therefore, the primary reason why God instituted the marriage covenant was for His image to be reflected.

The other reason why God instituted the marriage covenant is clearly said in the other verses of Genesis Chapter 2. God commanded Adam and Eve to be fruitful, multiply and fill the whole earth. In other words, God gave Adam and Eve the ability to procreate through sex and fill the earth with their offspring. In this instance, it is clear that God sanctions sex only to married couples for celebrating God's love and procreation.

There are a lot of people who regard sex as something not permitted by God. Perhaps these people are right because sex has been perverted a lot. Once it is done outside marriage, it becomes a sin. Since God's purpose for marriage is procreation, it becomes evident that same-sex marriage is not for God. God, in His wisdom, ordained humans not just to procreate for the fun of it; instead, there is a reason, which I shall discuss in chapter 2.

In conclusion, God instituted the marriage covenant to fulfil two purposes. The first one is to reflect the image of God.

The image of God is only reflected in a male and a female united in a holy institution called marriage. As long as the marriage institution reflects the image of God, there is no sin that can penetrate it. In a secondary sense, God purposefully designed the marriage to gain victory over sin.

The other reason why God instituted marriage was for humans to procreate through the gift of sex. The reason why God wants so many humans on Earth, all reflecting His image, will be discussed in chapter 2.

So, God created human beings in this order: He created Adam first and gave him his roles. He later caused Adam to sleep deeply and used his rib to create Eve. Adam had no say either in his creation, or in the creation of Eve, or in the handing over of Eve to him as his wife. All he did was express unspeakable joy at the sight of Eve.

Here are the reasons why God created them in that specific order. God created Adam first to ordain him as the head and the leader of Eve. He then gave him his roles before Eve was there so that there could be no confusion as to which roles Adam was to perform in his new home. Eve was then created to give Adam fulfilment and satisfy the vacuum created by her absence. This allowed emotional attachment, which was inseparable. As long as Adam and Eve would remain in the order and purpose of God, no gates of hell would prevail over them.

2| Pre or Post Fall

Ezekiel 28:13 – *Thou hast been in Eden, the garden of God; every precious stone was thy covering, the sardius, topaz, and the diamond, the beryl, the onyx, and the jasper, the sapphire, the emerald, and the carbuncle, and gold: the workmanship of thy tabrets and of thy pipes was prepared in thee in the day that thou wast created.*
28:14 – *Thou art the anointed cherub that covereth; and I have set thee so: thou wast upon the holy mountain of God; thou hast walked up and down in the midst of the stones of fire.*
28:15 – *Thou wast perfect in thy ways from the day that thou wast created, till iniquity was found in thee.*
Isaiah 14:12 – *How art thou fallen from heaven, O Lucifer, son of the morning! How art thou cut down to the ground, which didst weaken the nations!*
14:13 – *For thou hast said in thine heart, I will ascend into heaven, I will exalt my throne above the stars of God: I will sit also upon the mount of the congregation, in the sides of the north:*
14:14 – *I will ascend above the heights of the clouds; I will be like the most High.*
Revelation
12:7 – *And there was war in heaven: Michael and his angels fought against the dragon; and the dragon and his angels fought back.*
12:8 – *And prevailed not; neither was their place found any more in heaven.*
12:9 – *And the great dragon was cast out, that old serpent, called the Devil, and Satan, which deceiveth the whole world: he was cast out into the earth, and his angels were cast out with him.*

Revelation
12:4 – *And his tail drew the third part of the stars of heaven, and did cast them to the earth: and the dragon stood before the woman which was ready to be delivered, for to devour her child as soon as it was born.*
Genesis 3:1 – *Now the serpent was more subtle than any beast of the field which the LORD God had made. And he said unto the woman, "Yea, hath God said, 'Ye shall not eat of every tree of the garden?'"*
3:2 – *And the woman said unto the serpent, "We may eat of the fruit of the trees of the garden:*
3:3 – *But of the fruit of the tree which is in the midst of the garden, God hath said, 'Ye shall not eat of it, neither shall ye touch it, lest ye die.' "*
3:4 – *And the serpent said unto the woman, "Ye shall not surely die:*
3:5 – *For God doth know that in the day ye eat thereof, then your eyes shall be opened, and ye shall be as gods, knowing good and evil."*
3:6 – *And when the woman saw that the tree was good for food and that it was pleasant to the eyes, and a tree to be desired to make one wise, she took of the fruit thereof, and did eat, and gave also unto her husband with her; and he did eat.*
Genesis 3:24 – *So he drove out the man; and he placed at the east of the Garden of Eden Cherubims, and a flaming sword which turned every way, to keep the way of the tree of life.*
Genesis 3:14 – *And the LORD God said unto the serpent, "Because thou hast done this, thou art cursed above all cattle, and above every beast of the field; upon thy belly shalt thou go, and dust shalt thou eat all the days of thy life:*
3:15 – *And I will put enmity between thee and the woman, and between thy seed and her seed; it shall bruise thy head, and thou shalt bruise his heel."*

3:16 – *Unto the woman, he said, "I will greatly multiply thy sorrow and thy conception; in sorrow, thou shalt bring forth children; and thy desire shall be to thy husband, and he shall rule over thee."*
3:17 – *And unto Adam, he said, "Because thou hast hearkened unto the voice of thy wife, and hast eaten of the tree, of which I commanded thee, saying, Thou shalt not eat of it: cursed is the ground for thy sake; in sorrow shalt thou eat of it all the days of thy life;*
3:18 – *Thorns also and thistles shall it bring forth to thee; and thou shalt eat the herb of the field;*
3:19 – *In the sweat of thy face shalt thou eat bread, till thou return unto the ground; for out of it wast thou taken: for dust thou art, and unto dust shalt thou return."*

There is one reason why God created the planet Earth and subsequently created marriage. The reason is found in the books of Isaiah and Ezekiel. There was a rebellion in heaven caused by a created angel called Lucifer. Because of the beauty and many talents that the Lord God had bestowed upon him, he became proud of himself. He became proud to such an extent that he desired to be worshipped by other angels. He desired to be like God. He desired to set up his own government, which was better than God's government. He could not humble himself before his Creator. He refused to abide by God's law. He refused to respect the order that the God of heaven had put in place to preserve peace and unity in heaven. Lucifer reasoned that God's law cannot be kept. He reasoned that if the angels were free moral agencies, then why should they not worship any other being like God? He reasoned that since he had almost the same powers as God, he also deserved to be worshipped. He reasoned that he was going to lead a far better government than God, and all the angels who would come under his leadership would enjoy much more freedom than they had. Lucifer became the originator of sin, and he turned himself into a devil.

A closer look at the Book of Revelation will reveal that the devil was selling his ideas to the angels whom God had entrusted him to lead. Unfortunately, one-third of the heavenly angels supported the idea of Lucifer, and war broke out in heaven. The war was not easy then, and it is not easy now. It is called *the great controversy*. Even the angels who remained loyal to God, the creator, were not sure whether the devil had a point or not. This issue had to be settled to the satisfaction of all the heavenly intelligence. God was not going to resolve the issue by destroying the devil, as some might have suggested. Rather, He was going to make matters worse. Other angels might reason that perhaps, after all, Lucifer was correct, and that's why God destroyed him. So, God decided in His wisdom to address the issue by creating Earth. Some people think that Earth was created at the same time as other planets in the universe. But this is not true. The Bible clearly states that the sons of God (angels) sang with joy when Earth was created. Before this planet was created, there was already heaven.

There were angels who were going about God's business. Perhaps we should be reminded that the earth is just a small object in God's vast creation. And on that small object called the earth, God decided to settle the great controversy between himself and the devil. The whole universe was watching the drama unfold on planet Earth, and at the end of it all, God's character of love was vindicated, while the devil's intentions were revealed. The whole universe was given the chance to choose who to follow: God, the creator, or the devil, the creature. Therefore, the primary purpose of God creating planet Earth was to vindicate His character before the universe.

On planet Earth, God created human beings who are a little lower than the angels. Remember, the devil had declared that even angels cannot keep God's law. By creating human beings who are a little lower than the angels, God, in His wisdom, was demonstrating that even human beings who are lesser than the angels can keep the law as long as they abide by Him. Had Adam and Eve and their families kept the law as was prescribed by God, the contest would have been over a long time ago. Humans would have been elevated to the position of angels at the end of their probation. The only purpose of God creating Adam and Eve (marriage) was to fight sin. Just as the cell in the human body is the single unit to prevent diseases from entering the body, the family unit is the single unit that God made to prevent sin from entering the planet.

However, remember that the newly created planet and the newly blessed couple had no sin, although sin existed somewhere. The devil had rebelled against his creator and had sinned. He had also infected about one-third of the angles with sin. Since the righteous God does not dwell with sin, the devil lost the war in heaven and was hurled down. He wandered from one planet to the other, looking for more of God's creatures to infect with the virus called sin. The devil took notice of the newly created planet and the happiness of Adam and Eve and decided that he was going to cause them to sin against God and win them and the planet to his side. He decided that after winning the couple over, he would set up his own government on planet Earth.

The Lord God had given the law to Adam. As long as the family would remain faithful to God's law, no sin would defile them. But if they listened to the voice of the deceiver and broke the law of God, they would surely die. The law of God was introduced into the Garden of Eden as the tree of the knowledge of good and evil. God desired Adam and Eve to know only the good and did not want them to be exposed to the evil that had been experienced in heaven.

The reason why God made marriage is clear: to prevent sin from entering into humanity by keeping God's law. Marriage was to reflect God's image and demonstrate to the sinless worlds that it was possible to keep God's law. If our marriages depart from this primary purpose, God will be displeased, and the devil will be pleased.

For marriage to successfully prevent sin from entering humanity, there were important principles that had to be followed. The first important principle was for Adam and Eve to function in the order in which they were created by God. Since Adam was created by God first, he was to be the head of his wife. The other principle is that since the law of God was given to Adam, he had to remain the spiritual head or the priest of the family, and Eve was to remain the suitable helper for her husband. The pair had to adhere to the roles and functions they had been given by God. This formula was critical to follow because it was also like that in heaven. In heaven, there was God the Father, God the Son and God the Holy Spirit. These three co-eternal persons make one being called God. These three have different and specific roles, yet are united for one goal. This order is the one that was distorted by the devil when he desired the position of God, and it resulted in a catastrophe called sin.

The image of God the Father, God the Son and God the Holy Spirit was put into the marriage by God, the creator. Remember, the image was in the two – male and female – and not forgetting the third element of procreation through sex, which is represented by the Holy Spirit. Since the unity of God the Father, God the Son and God the Holy Spirit conquered the devil in heaven, it cannot be overemphasised that the unity of Adam and Eve and their offspring was going to conquer sin on earth. A clear point to note is that as long as Adam and Eve functioned in the order and roles that were prescribed by God, they would conquer sin. Any deviation from that would be a deviation from the law and order of God and would automatically allow sin to enter.

It, therefore, follows that the entrance of sin on the earth was due to the reversal of the order of creation by Adam and Eve. It is unfortunate because God had forewarned them. They were very clear that there was rebellion in heaven and that the devil had been thrown down. They were aware that the devil wanted to entice all God's creation into sin, including them. They were especially aware that they had to prevent the devil from entering the newly created planet, and they knew the formula. They were to live with what the Lord had said, and the family had to function in the roles prescribed by the Creator.

A sad thing happened in the Garden of Eden. Eve migrated from the side of her husband and found herself in conversation with the serpent. The conversation was not ordinary. It was based on their very existence in the Garden of Eden. The result of the conversation was either for life or for death. The subject upon which the snake was asking was not Eve's domain; it was Adam's. Eve should have been afraid to attempt to answer such a question concerning the tree of the knowledge of good and evil. After all, God gave the commandment to Adam and not to her. She was supposed to, with haste, call her husband to see how he would deal with the insinuations made by the serpent concerning the law of God. Instead, she felt confident in dealing with matters that did not concern her, and in that, she took the role of priesthood. She took the role of her husband, and the devil gained ground.

She even decided to eat the fruit before consulting Adam. When she had finished eating, she gave some to her husband, who also ate. Eve was deceived by the snake into eating the fruit, but Adam made the decision to eat on his own. He decided to die with his wife. He loved her so much that he could not even think of living without Eve. He applied the "till death do us part" rule and decided to die with Eve. He took the fruit and ate it, and from then onwards, the human race on the earth fell into sin and the whole package that it brought. Some people actually doubt whether it was the reversal of the roles that led the couple into sin, but there is enough evidence in the Book of Genesis to support this view.

After God had looked for Adam and Eve to understand what had taken place, He decided to give a punishment suited for the three of them who were involved. Of interest is the punishment that was given to Eve. She was to continue bearing children – the role she had been given before sin entered the Garden of Eden – but now she would do so with much pain. The last part of the punishment is startling. Eve's desires should be upon her husband, and Adam had to rule over her. A closer look at these "punishments" would reveal that these were not punishments but redemptive solutions. Remember, God had not given up on the human race, as we shall see shortly. What he was doing was giving the couple the solution to the sin problem that had just entered their life. To Eve, God was saying, "You did not stay in your position as the wife of Adam and ventured to speak to the snake, which you were not supposed to do, and this eventually allowed sin to enter. Now, I want to remind you that from now on, Adam will not only be the head and the priest, but he shall also rule over you, and your desires should be subjected to Adam's authority." Therefore, the position of Adam as the head and the priest of Eve was re-emphasised. If Eve had submitted to Adam's authority and respected his role as the priest and the head, this would have prevented the recurrence of sin in their family.

What caused sin to enter the Garden of Eden was the reversal of roles, and what could prevent it was the restoration of the same order, which was only this time with more emphasis. The redemptive solutions that were given to the remaining two were also the same. There was nothing to restore the snake: Jesus would come to crush its head. To Adam, the issue of work was emphasised. God had given Adam the role of caring for his environment as he continued learning more about God. He would continue to do the same, but this time he would sweat. The more he would sweat, the more he would be reminded about the entrance and existence of sin on the planet. He would keep on working for God and for his family until the serpent's head was crushed.

There was also a clue in the Book of Genesis that showed that the issue of roles was critical. After sin entered the earth, God came down to the garden in the cool of the day to investigate the matter. God knew very well that Eve was at fault in this matter, but God did not look for Eve. He looked for Adam. God called, "Adam, Adam, where are you?" The reason why God called Adam is very clear: He had given the law to Adam, and He demanded accountability for the entrance of sin from Adam. The office to defend the word of God and lead the family in righteousness was not given to Eve; it was given to Adam. Since Adam allowed Eve to wander away from him and converse with the snake, he was responsible for the catastrophe of sin in the family and on the planet.

The devil thought he had won. He wanted the entire universe, including the angels who remained in heaven and those who had refused to follow him, to see. He said that God was a tyrannical ruler and that His laws were taxing and no one could keep the law. He pointed at Adam and Eve, crowing that they had failed to keep the law and now belonged to him.

But the God of heaven had other plans. He did not abandon His people, for to abandon His creation was to succumb to the devil. Despite the fact that sin existed in the universe and now had penetrated the earth, God, through the principle of love, remained resolute in dealing with the devil. When the promise to crush the head of the serpent was given in the Garden of Eden, it was clear that the great controversy was not over, and the battle would take place on planet Earth. The battles would be for God or the devil in and through families. Therefore, God gave hope to Adam. Instead of sewing fig leaves to cover them, He killed an animal and covered them with its skin. God would cover them Himself with His garments of righteousness. They were to do nothing, for the battle was not theirs, but since they allowed the sin to enter, the battle would be fought through them. All they needed to do was to do what they failed to do in the first place. They would adhere to the order given in Eden, for it was meant to prevent the entrance of sin. They would keep the law of God, for it is the one they broke. They would believe in the One who would die for them, for they would no longer die themselves. If only they believed in the coming saviour, they would be restored to their original estate as though they had not sinned.

Henceforth, Adam and Eve abided by the word of God and preached the coming saviour to their children as their only source of hope. They regretted having broken God's law, but they were thankful that they had been given a second chance, and they took the chance. The Lord protected the tree of life with angels of fire so that no descendant of Adam could eat from it and become immortal sinners. He drove them out of the Garden, and they began to realise how grave the sin was. Anyway, they managed to eat from the tree and clung to the hope of the Messiah to such an extent that they thought their first son, Cain, could be the one. But the world had to wait until the time was fully cupped. God removed the tree of life from the Garden of Eden and took it to heaven, and when the great controversy will be over, those who will be found in the Book of Life will have access to the tree of life, family-by-family.

Did God abandon the objectives for creating a family? No, no, no. The family remains the centre where the battle against sin is fought. God designed humanity to be made holy through and in families. Therefore, the husband should take his position, and so should the wife as the great controversy continues. Planet Earth becomes the theatre, the spectacle, as the sinless worlds expect the war to be ended, for the greater part of it was fought on the cross, and the sinless worlds have anchored their decision on Christ after the devil's intentions were exposed on the cross.

3| Order in Heaven and on Earth: An Organogram

Psalms
119:160 – *Thy word is true from the beginning: and every one of thy righteous judgments endureth forever.*
Matthew
5:18 – *For verily I say unto you, "Till heaven and earth pass, one jot or one tittle shall in no wise pass from the law, till all be fulfilled."*
1 John 3:4 – *Whosoever committeth sin transgresseth also the law: for sin is the transgression of the law.*
1 Corinthians
11:3 – *But I would have you know, that the head of every man is Christ; and the head of the woman is the man; and the head of Christ is God.*
11:7 – *For a man indeed ought not to cover his head, forasmuch as he is the image and glory of God: but the woman is the glory of the man.*
11:8 – *For the man is not of the woman; but the woman of the man.*
11:9 – *Neither was the man created for the woman; but the woman for the man.*
11:11 – *Nevertheless neither is the man without the woman, neither the woman without the man, in the Lord.*
11:12 – *For as the woman is of the man, even so is the man also by the woman; but all things of God.*
Genesis 2:19 – *And out of the ground the LORD God formed every beast of the field, and every fowl of the air; and brought them unto Adam to see what he would call them: and whatsoever Adam called every living creature, that was the name thereof.*

2:20 – *And Adam gave names to all cattle, and to the fowl of the air, and to every beast of the field; but for Adam, there was not found any helper for him.*

2:21 – *And the LORD God caused a deep sleep to fall upon Adam, and he slept: and he took one of his ribs, and closed up the flesh instead thereof;* 2:22 - *And the rib, which the LORD God had taken from man, made he a woman, and brought her unto the man.*

2:23 – *And Adam said, "This is now bone of my bones and flesh of my flesh: she shall be called Woman because she was taken out of Man.*

Ephesians

5:22 – *Wives, submit yourselves unto your own husbands, as unto the Lord.*

5:23 – *For the husband is the head of the wife, even as Christ is the head of the church: and he is the saviour of the body.*

5:24 – *Therefore, as the church is subject unto Christ, let the wives be to their own husbands in everything.*

God has designed order as necessary for any government to function properly. This concept has been adopted here on earth by our earthly governments. There are offices that are protected by the constitution regardless of the type of person who occupies the office. The office itself makes the occupier as sacred as the constitution itself. For this order to prevail, these offices have to be protected by the constitution. The constitution becomes the law.

In heaven, order and protocol have always been maintained by the Law. The Law of God has always been there. The law is as old as the Creator Himself. The book of Psalms magnifies the concept that the law of God is eternal. Matthew concurs and adds that heaven and earth may pass away, but there is no jot that will pass away from the law. The reason why the law cannot be done away with is very simple: where there is no law, there is chaos. Imagine a country where there is no law. Any person can kill anyone, and no one will be arrested. Anyone can kill, steal, or do whatever they want, and no one will be prosecuted or punished. That kind of country is not safe to live in, and no one in his or her senses would like to stay in such a country. Therefore, God designed the law to govern His universe in order for the universe to enjoy peace and freedom. This is why breaking God's law is a sin that is punishable only by death.

The book of Romans points out that the wages of sin is death. This is what started the war in heaven. In heaven, there was peace and tranquillity. There was harmony. God's creation was at rest. This is what is known as *Sabbatismos*. *Sabbatismos* prevailed in heaven until Lucifer broke God's law. Lucifer sinned in heaven, and there was war. There was no more peace, no more rest. There was chaos. Some people are not sure which law the devil broke. The devil broke the whole law of the universe. Take, for example, the first law in the Ten Commandments, which says – *thou shall not worship other gods before Me*. Lucifer broke this very first commandment. The book of Isaiah and Ezekiel points out that Lucifer was so proud in his heart that he decided to take his position above that of his creator. He decided to be worshipped. He decided to be the god of heaven apart from God, the creator.

What of the commandment which says – *thou shall not take the name of the Lord your God in vain*? Did not Lucifer break this one, too? Lucifer decided to go about all heaven, where he had influence, and start a campaign against the government of God. He despised God's law and thereby despised His office. He created chaos in heaven. There was confusion among the heavenly hosts because of the disorder that was created by Satan. Order and peace were restored only when the devil was thrown out of heaven.

It is critical for Christians to realise that order is the first law of heaven. To disregard God's law of order is equivalent to sin. It means you are taking the side of the devil in the great controversy. The order of heaven was further explained by Paul. Paul explained that the head of Christ is God in heaven. The devil tried to distort this order and his place was not found in heaven.

It is crucial to note that God desired the same order to be maintained on the earth. When God created the marriage order, He deliberately instilled order. The image of God in the male and female was reflected by the order God instilled in the marriage. Paul explained that the order of the earth starts with Christ Himself. The head of the man (husband) is Christ, and the head of the woman (wife) is the man. God designed this order for a purpose. It was not a suggestion. The woman was given the role of being the suitable helper for the husband, bearing children and raising them in the fear of God. Just like men, women are called to evangelise through various ways that respect and maintain God's order, but their main field is in their homes. Their first converts should be their children. This does not mean that men are less involved as home missionaries, but in addition to that, they have a wider field in the church, as we shall explore.

In Genesis, God followed these steps to emphasise the importance of order in the family:

- Adam was created first, before Eve.
- Adam was given the Garden of Eden to till before Eve was created. This implies that the duties of working and providing for the family are primarily Adam's.
- The commandment not to eat from the tree of the knowledge of good and evil in the middle of the garden was given to Adam. This implies that the spiritual head in the marriage is the man. The duty to

defend the marriage from false teachings and the doctrinal attacks from the devil is primarily Adam's.

- Adam was given the duty to give names to all inanimate and animate creatures in the Garden of Eden before Eve was created. This implies that Adam was given the role of decision-making in the marriage. Most people, especially those who are gender-sensitive, do not like this point, but it is common knowledge that, even in the secular world, there are CEOs and chairpersons in companies. This is important for order and the smooth running of organisations. It is so with marriage. The husband, as the chairperson, is the one who makes decisions for the family. He is there to be the head, lead, moderate, and listen to the views of the whole family. Where decisions are difficult to make, the husband must consult his head, who is Jesus Christ. Let's not forget that the head of the husband is Christ, and if this order is maintained, no husband will oppress his family.
- Finally, God made Adam sleep and created Eve out of his (Adam's) rib. This implies that Adam's greatest task was to treat Eve as his own flesh and love her. The two - if they had maintained the order of creation, with Christ as the head of the husband - together with their offspring would have reflected the image of God.

Wives are to submit to their own husbands as unto the Lord. The wife is a representative of the church. The church that does not submit to Christ is an apostate church. The wife who does not submit to her husband is an apostate wife. Submission does not mean that women are inferior to men, for men are called to do much more than submit. They are called to die for their wives, just as Christ died for His church. This kind of model will become the image of Christ and the church in a marriage. Christ exhibited all those characteristics. He loved the church while it was still in sin. He humbled and submitted Himself even to His death on the cross. Submission in a wife and love in a husband will complete the picture of Christ in a marriage. Wives are called on to submit not to take an inferior role to that of men but rather to become redeemable, for the lack of submission allowed Eve to talk to the snake before consulting her husband. Men are called to love their wives as their own flesh and make them redeemable, for Adam's action to allow Eve to wander from him and make decisions on his behalf was a lack of vigilance and love. Thus, through the commandment of submission and love, God is trying to supply what is lacking in males and females to complete His image in a marriage.

4| Marriage to Conquer Sin: The Image Concept

John 10:30 – *I and my Father are one.*
John 1:1 – *In the beginning was the Word, and the Word was with God, and the Word was God.*
1:2 – *The same was in the beginning with God.*
1:3 – *All things were made by him; and without him was not anything made that was made.*
John 12:49 – *For I have not spoken of myself; but the Father which sent me, he gave me a commandment, what I should say, and what I should speak.*
John 14:26 – *But the Comforter, which is the Holy Ghost, whom the Father will send in my name, he shall teach you all things, and bring all things to your remembrance, whatsoever I have said unto you.*
Philippians
2:5 – *Let this mind be in you, which was also in Christ Jesus:*
2:6 – *Who, being in the form of God, thought it not robbery to be equal with God:*
2:7 – *But made himself of no reputation, and took upon him the form of a servant, and was made in the likeness of men:*
2:8 – *And being found in fashion as a man, he humbled himself and became obedient unto death, even the death of the cross.*
1 Corinthians
11:3 – *But I would have you know, that the head of every man is Christ; and the head of the woman is the man; and the head of Christ is God.*
11:4 – *Every man praying or prophesying, having his head covered, dishonoureth his head.*

11:5 – *But every woman that prayeth or prophesieth with her head uncovered dishonoureth her head: for that is even all one as if she were shaven.*

11:6 – *For if the woman be not covered, let her also be shorn: but if it be a shame for a woman to be shorn or shaven, let her be covered.*

11:7 – *For a man indeed ought not to cover his head, for as much as he is the image and glory of God: but the woman is the glory of the man.*

11:8 – *For the man is not of the woman; but the woman of the man.*

11:9 – *Neither was the man created for the woman, but the woman for the man.*

11:10 – *For this cause ought the woman to have power on her head because of the angels.*

11:11 – *Nevertheless neither is the man without the woman, neither the woman without the man, in the Lord.*

11:12 – *For as the woman is of the man, even so is the man also by the woman; but all things of God.*

Ephesians

5:22 – *Wives, submit yourselves unto your own husbands, as unto the Lord.*

5:23 – *For the husband is the head of the wife, even as Christ is the head of the church: and he is the saviour of the body.*

5:24 – *Therefore as the church is subject unto Christ, so let the wives be to their own husbands in everything.*

5:25 – *Husbands, love your wives, even as Christ also loved the church, and gave himself for it;*

5:26 – *That he might sanctify and cleanse it with the washing of water by the word,*

5:27 – *That he might present it to himself a glorious church, not having spot, or wrinkle, or any such thing; but that it should be holy and without blemish.*

5:28 – *So ought men to love their wives as their own bodies. He that loveth his wife loveth himself.*
5:29 – *For no man ever yet hated his own flesh; but nourisheth and cherisheth it, even as the Lord the church:*
5:30 – *For we are members of his body, of his flesh, and of his bones.*
5:31 – *For this cause shall a man leave his father and mother and shall be joined unto his wife, and they two shall be one flesh.*
5:32 – *This is a great mystery: but I speak concerning Christ and the church.*

Law and order are the pillars of heaven, and they shall remain so forever and ever! Amen. They have preserved peace, order and harmony in heaven. The harmonious function of the Godhead must be the object of study here on earth. Three co-eternal persons make up what is called God: God the Father, God the Son and God the Holy Spirit.

These three are perfectly equal in worth and are united in one purpose. Jesus Himself testified that He and the Father are one. What this means is that you cannot separate the Son from the Father. They are perfectly equal. The book of John points out that in the beginning, there was the word. We understand that this word was Jesus because He is eventually the one who incarnated to become flesh and came here on earth to reveal the glory of the Father. The same book continues to say that this word (Jesus) was with God. In other words, Jesus has always been part of the Godhead. John further clarifies that this word (Jesus) was God. Therefore, there is no distinction between God the Father and God the Son. It is the same with the Holy Spirit; He is fully God.

Yet it is very interesting to see that these three are also different. They are different in roles and functions. God the Father is the head of Jesus, while Jesus has the power to send the Holy Spirit. In terms of roles and functions, the

Father is the greatest of the three, followed by Jesus and then the Holy Spirit. God the Son (Jesus) is not a lesser deity because He is the Son. He remains fully God. It is clear that Jesus was humble enough to submit to the authority of the Father and was the one who took the role of dying for the human race after the Eden catastrophe. That's why He is God the Son. He is not the biological son of the Father, but the one who was sent, and the title 'God the Son' will allow us to understand that.

It is the same with the Holy Spirit. Jesus told His disciples that He would ask the Father to send them the Holy Spirit in His name (Jesus' Name). He further explained that the duty of the Holy Spirit is to remind the world of all that Jesus had taught them. Therefore, the Holy Spirit is a perfect representation of Jesus on earth. While Jesus is perfectly happy to do the Father's will, so also is the Holy Spirit. It is crucial at this moment to note that there was one son who was not willing to submit himself to the order of heaven. That was Lucifer, who turned himself into the devil. God (Father, Son and Holy Spirit) is perfectly united to accomplish the one purpose of saving humankind. None of them will divert by the minutest inch from this goal.

So, God created the couple (male and female) in His image. The image of God should be reflected in the equality of male and female as it is in the equality which is the Godhead. God created Adam first. From there, He created Eve from Adam's rib. The rib was on the side of Adam and not on the head or on the foot. This denotes that Adam was not to be ruled over by Eve, nor was he to trample her under his foot. He was to treat her as his equal. The other point is that Eve was created from the flesh of Adam, meaning that the two were one flesh. Eve was an extension of Adam. Paul pointed to the fact that the man is not of the woman, but the woman is of the man. In other words, Eve is the one who was created from

Adam and for Adam. But Paul quickly mentioned that the man was nothing without the woman, and the woman was nothing without the man. Paul was addressing the issue of equality here. Both males and females are important to each other in the Lord. Neither of them is less important than the other despite the order of creation.

The image of God is also seen in the functions and roles. From the book of Genesis, the Lord God created man first and gave him the commandment. In this case, God established Adam as the head of the woman and the spiritual leader. That was before the entrance of sin into the garden. However, even after the entrance of sin into planet Earth, Adam's role did not change. In fact, it became even more established. God told Eve that her husband would rule over her and that her desires should be to her husband. God emphasised this in order for the couple to be redeemable. Eve, as a God-fearing woman who had fallen into sin and was now aware of the consequences of sin, gladly accepted this role from her Creator, and nothing has ever been mentioned suggesting that Eve had any complaints concerning this God-assigned role. She perfectly discharged her duties in the fear of the Lord and her husband.

Paul also wrote to the Corinthians concerning these God-given roles. Some would like to paint the picture that the society in which Paul lived was male-dominated, and hence his writings, but that is not true. What Paul was writing was from the book of Genesis, when God created heaven and earth and ordained marriage, which was long before Paul's society came into existence. Paul told the Corinthians that the head of Jesus is God the Father, the head of the man is Jesus, and the head of the wife is the man. This is from God, and it should be adhered to. The husband is the head of the wife. Remember, God the Father and God the Son are perfectly equal, but for the sake of discharging the roles and functions, God the

Father is the head of Christ. In the same way, the husband and the wife are equal; they are worth the same in the eyes of God, but in terms of roles and functions, the husband is the head of the wife.

To the Christians at Ephesus, Paul emphasised the same issue, but this time he added another dimension. He pointed out that the man is the head of the wife, as Christ is the head of the church. This simply means that God also put the image of Christ and the church in the marriage. In this instance, the man represents Jesus, while the woman represents the church. This image should be kept in view, for I shall visit it later. For the marriage to work for the purpose for which God created it, a woman should submit herself to her husband. Just as Christ was willing to submit and to be sent by the Father, the wife should be happy and willing to submit to her husband. Christ did not hold to Him being equal with God, though He was fully God; He was willing to humble Himself. A wife should not hold to her being equal with the husband. She must realise that she has a role to perform in the Godly marriage and must be willing to submit herself to her husband in the fear of the Lord. After Christ humbled Himself even to the death on the cross, the Father raised Him and elevated Him to the position above every power and principality in heaven, on earth and in the sea below. After humility comes power. A wife who is willing to submit herself to her husband will be uplifted by God to raise a family waiting to meet Jesus. She will be endowed with power from on high, and that is true women empowerment.

Paul does not end with women. He continues to give admonitions as he turns to men. Men should love their wives as Christ loves the church. This concept will be explored further in the coming chapters. In a nutshell, however, a man should realise that his wife is part of his flesh. No one hates his flesh. No one abuses his flesh. Everyone looks after and nourishes his flesh. If the wife submits herself to her husband and the husband loves his wife as his own flesh, no marriage will fail. The husband and wife, being equal in the eyes of God, should function in the roles they were given by God. They should perform different roles for one purpose: to overcome sin. They should function to meet the objective of the Godhead, which is their salvation. In this way, the marriage will reflect the image of God. When a marriage fails to function in the roles ordained by God, and the husband and wife fail to unite for one purpose, that is, worshipping God, the marriage will fail to reflect the image of God and will become a habitation of demons.

It is unfortunate that Bible-believing Christians have adopted women empowerment as envisioned by the secular world as the solution to the problems that families are experiencing. Christians who have such a beautiful model of running their homes have stooped so low as to adopt equal rights as portrayed by the world. The Bible has given sufficient guidelines on how families should be run, and if equal rights and empowerment are not addressed according to what the Bible says, they will not bring solutions to family problems. The so-called women empowerment is actually women dethronement. Humanity, while looking for solutions that have not been designed by God, has fallen farther away from God than when sin entered the Garden of Eden, making it difficult for the Saviour to reach us. This is counterfeit women empowerment and has been empowered by the devil. Women who refuse to submit to their husbands in the fear of the Lord will become the representatives of the devil. Remember, the devil is the one who refused to submit to the authority of God.

Husbands who do not love their wives as their own flesh will become the representatives of the devil, for there is no love that comes from the devil. In the same vein, husbands who love their wives as their own flesh will become representatives of Christ in the home. Wives who are submissive to their husbands will become a symbol of the church, which has accepted the love of Christ and abides in His love. The purpose of God the Father will be accomplished from heaven down to here on earth.

From God the Father, who is the head of Christ, to God the Son; from God the Son, to the man who is the head of the woman through the Holy Spirit; from the husband, who is the head of the woman, to the wife; and from the wife to the children: this order is paramount. Women who reject this order will produce the offspring of the devil. Instead of procreating the Godly seed, they will give birth to tyrants such as Emperor Nero, Herod and Hitler, to mention a few. They will breed murderers, adulterers, fornicators, lovers of money, lovers of their own selves, covetous boasters, proud blasphemers, children who are disobedient to their parents, unthankful, unholy, without natural affection, trucebreakers, false accusers, people who are incontinent, fierce, despisers of those who are good, traitors, heady, high-minded lovers of pleasures, people with the form of godliness, but denying the power thereof. Women who refuse to follow God's order will be themselves perpetrators of abuse instead of ending it and will end up taking the side of the devil in the great controversy.

It should be noted that abuse cannot be put to an end by human rights and women's rights groups. Abuse is a symptom of sin. It can only be put to an end when families receive Christ and live with a "thus said the Lord."

Abuse is not a disease like malaria, which needs rigorous campaigns and distribution of drugs and mosquito nets. Abuse is a symptom of sin, which can only cured by Jesus. For as long as marriages are inspired by human rights activists instead of the Bible, the results are always going to be the same: abuse, pain, suffering and ultimately death, even eternal death.

5| Divorce is an Abomination

Genesis 2:24 – *Therefore shall a man leave his father and his mother, and shall cleave unto his wife: and they shall be one flesh.*

1 Corinthians

6:16 – *What? Know ye not that he which is joined to a harlot is one body? For two, saith he, shall be one flesh.*

6:17 – *But he that is joined unto the Lord is one spirit.*

6:18 – *Flee fornication. Every sin that a man doeth is without the body; but he that committeth fornication sinneth against his own body.*

Malachi

2:13 – *And this have ye done again, covering the altar of the LORD with tears, with weeping, and with crying out, insomuch that he regardeth not the offering any more, or receiveth it with good will at your hand.*

2:14 – *Yet ye say, "Wherefore?" Because the LORD hath been witness between thee and the wife of thy youth, against whom thou hast dealt treacherously: yet is she thy companion, and the wife of thy covenant.*

2:15 – *And did not he make one? Yet had he the residue of the spirit. And wherefore one? That he might seek a godly seed. Therefore, take heed to your spirit, and let none deal treacherously against the wife of his youth.*

2:16 – *For the LORD, the God of Israel, saith that he hateth putting away: for one covereth violence with his garment, saith the LORD of hosts: therefore take heed to your spirit, that ye deal not treacherously.*

Matthew
19:3 – *The Pharisees also came unto him, tempting him and saying unto him, "Is it lawful for a man to put away his wife for every cause?"*
19:4 – *And he answered and said unto them, "Have ye not read that he which made them at the beginning made them male and female?"*
19:5 – *And said, "For this cause shall a man leave father and mother, and shall cleave to his wife: and they twain shall be one flesh.*
19:6 – *Wherefore they are no more twain, but one flesh. What therefore God hath joined together, let not man put asunder."*
19:7 – *They said unto him, "Why did Moses then command to give a writing of divorcement, and to put her away?"*
19:8 – *He saith unto them, "Moses, because of the hardness of your hearts, suffered you to put away your wives: but from the beginning it was not so."*
19:9 – *And I say unto you, "Whosoever shall put away his wife, except it be for fornication, and shall marry another, committeth adultery: and whoso marrieth her which is put away doth commit adultery."*
Hosea 1:2 – *The beginning of the word of the LORD by Hosea. And the LORD said to Hosea, "Go, take unto thee a wife of whoredoms and children of whoredoms: for the land hath committed great whoredom, departing from the LORD."*
Hosea 3:1 – *Then said the LORD unto me, "Go yet, love a woman beloved of her friend, yet an adulteress, according to the love of the LORD toward the children of Israel, who look to other gods, and love flagons of wine."*
3:2 – *So I bought her to me for fifteen pieces of silver, and for a homer of barley, and a half homer of barley:*
3:3 – *And I said unto her, "Thou shalt abide for me many days; thou shalt not play the harlot, and thou shalt not be for another man: so will I also be for thee."*

3:4 – *For the children of Israel shall abide many days without a king, and without a prince, and without a sacrifice, and without an image, and without an ephod, and without teraphim:*
3:5 – *Afterward shall the children of Israel return, and seek the LORD their God, and David, their king; and shall fear the LORD and his goodness in the latter days.*

Divorce is no longer a thing that is scary in the society in which we live. Marriage has been torn apart by divorce. The statistics of divorce, as indicated in the introduction, are scary. 50% of the couples that marry end up divorcing. In the case of second and third marriages, the percentage even rises. In order not to be hurt by divorce, people have ended up inventing other ways of living together. Some of them have invented ways, such as cohabitation (where unmarried people stay together while keeping separate interests), while others do what is called *living in*. They make arrangements to stay together just for the purpose of fulfilling needs such as sexual needs. Sometimes, they make such arrangements to raise their children together. The only problem with these arrangements is that each partner is prepared to move out when they are hurt. It is sort of a contract.

Marriage, from the biblical perspective, is not a contract. It is a covenant. A contract can be terminated at any time if the conditions of the agreement are not met and the costs associated with the termination can be met. It is not so with marriage. Direct from the Creator, God has declared that marriage is permanent. The conditions of a covenant cannot be broken even if the conditions of the covenant are not met. A covenant involves blood, and as such, it can only be broken through death.

People may want to know where blood is involved in marriage. Blood is involved in every phase of marriage. First of all, the Lord God created Eve from the flesh of Adam. Therefore, through God's mystery, the couple who decides to get married will become one flesh. God declared this in the very beginning when He blessed marriage. He pronounced that the two that are married will become one flesh. What is flesh without blood? The union of husband and wife is by covenant of blood because they are one flesh.

Secondly, marriage is a blood covenant through the union of sex. Paul explains this whole issue by pointing out that he who is joined to a harlot becomes a harlot as well. Paul discusses this in the context of sex because, just below this statement, he urges Corinthian believers to flee fornication. Paul puts it in a way that is easy to understand. He points out that other sins are better than fornication (if sins are to be classified). The reason why other sins are better is because they happen outside the body. This means that they are very easy to leave if one decides to leave them. But adultery is very difficult to leave. This is because it involves blood. When you engage in sexual activity with a person, there is an exchange of blood. If that person has demons, you can have those demons. If that person is a harlot, you will also become a harlot. It is a mystery.

God designed sex to bind the two people together. Hence, it should only be done in the context of marriage. People should remember that sex was created by God, and it should be done in the context in which He created it. When people pervert the gift of sex as given by God, they come to believe that God is not involved in the sexual activities of His people. This is a deception from the devil. When people engage in sexual activities outside God's plan, that which God designed sex to achieve will still be achieved. Sex is designed to bind the couple in the covenant of blood. If it is done with partners possessed by demonic spirits, the two will share the same demonic spirit. Through sex, couples are bound by marriage in the covenant of blood.

The covenant of blood is also seen in the offspring that the couple produce. The blood of the wife and the blood of the husband are found in the children they bear. The blood of the couple will find common ground in their children. God could have chosen another way of reproduction rather than sex. He could have allowed us humans to do grafting, as we do with some types of plants. He could have allowed children to grow from our fingers; after all, there are other animal species that propagate through cell division. Sex is a unique experience, and sexual perversion is a sin of the highest order.

From that backdrop, it follows that no human being is allowed to break the covenant of marriage. The statement from God Himself made it clear: "What God joins together, let no man put asunder." God hates divorce. Malachi gives a clear picture. God had enough spirit to create more than one wife for Adam. But He made only one wife for Adam because He was seeking a Godly seed. Therefore, it follows that a married couple that is not two (one wife, one husband) cannot produce a Godly seed. A marriage that is made up of partners of the same sex or is polygamous or any marriage where the arrangements do not fit in God's design cannot produce a Godly seed. It is clear that God's aim in instituting marriage was for humanity to seek God and be righteous.

God hates divorce because it is a misrepresentation of His character. Divorce will completely obliterate the image of God that He put in the marriage from the beginning. The Bible says, "So God created man in his own image, in the image of God created he him; male and female created he them." So where does divorce leave the image of God in the male and female?

Divorce also distorts the plan of salvation as represented by the marriage. In marriage, the husband represents Christ, while the wife represents the church. Like God, who loved the church so much that he died for it, the husband should love his wife so much that he will sacrifice anything for her. The business of the husband should be his wife, just as the business of Jesus is to look after the church; everything He has done and is doing is for the benefit of His church. A husband should love his wife with *agape* love. Love is not a feeling; it is a principle. A husband who truly loves his wife will not give conditions. He will adore his wife, provide for all the needs and wants of his wife, use all his resources to beautify and make his wife attractive, and attend to all disease problems that the wife may experience. He will love even a wife who is not loveable, has bad manners and is argumentative. A husband will be loving, joyful, peaceful, long-suffering, gentle, good, faithful, meek and temperate to his wife. When a husband reflects on the above traits when dealing with his wife, he represents the character of Jesus.

God showed His love to us even when we were sinners and died for us. A husband, like God, should show love to his wife even if she is imperfect and must sacrifice everything for her. A husband who truly loves his wife will never desert her when she is at the lowest point of her life; rather, he will rise up and stand in the position of Christ. This arrangement will not leave room for divorce in any circumstance. A husband should contemplate the love of Christ on the cross before he leads his family. If a husband considers giving up on the marriage, he must ask himself: "What if Christ had given up on me?" Is there a situation in life where God has given up on His people?

If God was in the habit of becoming fed up with His people, He could have been fed up with Abraham, Jacob, David and Solomon, to mention a few. God's covenant with His people can only be broken by death, but as we see, it is always the people who do not appreciate the love of God and decide to run away from Him and choose to die. But even under such circumstances, God continues to give His people a second, third, fourth – even a hundredth – chance. It is surprising these days how easily people give up on their marriages and fail to represent the love of God. When the husband decides to divorce his wife, it is like Christ who decides to give up on His church. Christ cannot give up on His church, whatever the circumstances. It is only the devil who lies to people that he loves them and, in the long run, he hurts them. A man who divorces his wife is a representative of the devil. Under no circumstances a marriage is allowed to be separated by divorce; a marriage can only be separated by death.

People are quick to quote the adultery clause. The adultery clause states that marriage partners are allowed to divorce if one of them commits adultery. This is not entirely correct. People should study the Hosea story. The story of Hosea was both literal and spiritual. Hosea was literally instructed by God to marry a harlot. We should keep in mind that marriage is an image of Christ and His Church. The way the innocent partner is hurt when there is adultery in the family is not as painful as the way God is hurt when the church commits adultery (breaks God's commandments). There is no human being who can feel the pain that Christ underwent when He was dying for His church. When God instructed Hosea to marry Goma, the harlot, God wanted to demonstrate to Israel that, even though Israel committed adultery with other gods, He still loved them and would never give up on them. It is also prudent to note that after Goma was married and bore children to Hosea, she decided to run away to commit adultery again. To Hosea's surprise, God instructed him to go and purchase Goma again. God demonstrated to Israel again that, even after repeated rejection of His love, God still loved them. In the literal sense, Hosea was supposed to forgive his wife, whom he had married, when she ran away again to play harlotry.

We cannot separate our marriages from representing Christ and the church, for in that context, God instituted and blessed the marriage covenant. Therefore, even in the event of adultery, before the partners consider divorce, they should consider forgiveness, for forgiveness is a divine trait. To err is human, and to forgive is divine.

Couples should not see the adultery clause as a route for divorce, for in it, there is no justification for divorce. However, this is not to say that a partner should regard forgiveness as a way that can give him/her leeway to commit adultery. Remember that sex is sacred, and it involves the sharing of blood. Having sex outside marriage is like having other covenants with other partners. It is like forming bonds with other people rather than your spouse, and, as Paul has already pointed out, sexual bonds are very difficult to break because they happen right inside the body. That is why God likens a church that does not keep His commandments to an adulterous church. Adultery is the last thing that should happen in marriage. It destroys everything that marriage stands for. It destroys; it kills. Thus, while forgiveness should be the first thing to consider when a marriage undergoes adultery, Christ Himself has given room for divorce under these circumstances.

6| Single But Not Gifted

Genesis 2:18 – *And the LORD God said, "It is not good that the man should be alone; I will make a helper for him."*

1 Corinthians

11:8 – *For the man is not of the woman; but the woman of the man.*

1 Timothy

5:9 – *Let not a widow be taken into the number under threescore years old, having been the wife of one man,*

5:10 – *Well reported of for good works; if she have brought up children, if she have lodged strangers, if she have washed the saints' feet, if she have relieved the afflicted, if she have diligently followed every good work.*

5:11 – *But the younger widows refuse: for when they have begun to wax wanton against Christ, they will marry;*

5:12 – *Having damnation, because they have cast off their first faith.*

5:13 – *And withal they learn to be idle, wandering about from house to house; and not only idle, but tattlers also and busybodies, speaking things which they ought not.*

5:14 – *I will therefore that the younger women marry, bear children, guide the house, give none occasion to the adversary to speak reproachfully.*

1 Corinthians

7:1 – *Now concerning the things whereof ye wrote unto me: It is good for a man not to touch a woman.*

7:2 – *Nevertheless, to avoid fornication, let every man have his own wife, and let every woman have her own husband.*

7:3 – *Let the husband render unto the wife due benevolence: and likewise also the wife unto the husband.*

7:4 – *The wife hath not power of her own body, but the husband: and likewise also the husband hath not power of his own body, but the wife.*
7:5 – *Defraud ye not one the other, except it be with consent for a time, that ye may give yourselves to fasting and prayer; and come together again, that Satan tempt you not for your incontinency.*
7:6 – *But I speak this by permission, and not of commandment.*
7:7 – *For I would that all men were even as I myself. But every man hath his proper gift of God, one after this manner, and another after that.*
7:8 – *I say therefore to the unmarried and widows it is good for them if they abide even as I.*
7:9 – *But if they cannot contain, let them marry: for it is better to marry than to burn.*
7:10 – *And unto the married I command yet not I, but the Lord, let not the wife depart from her husband:*

The first word that God uttered concerning marriage was that it is not good for a man to be alone. These words were uttered by the Creator, God. It was not Adam who suggested to God that it was not good for him to be alone. After all, Adam was not involved in creation and had no idea what God was going to create after him (Adam). It is important for people to realise that the matter of being alone (single) or having a companion (married) was not for Adam to decide. I have alluded to the fact that one of the reasons why God created humanity was for them to procreate. This was necessary for God to fill up the vacancies that were left in heaven by the devil and his angels when they rebelled against their creator. If Adam and Eve had conquered the temptation from the devil, together with their offspring, they could have been elevated to the status of angels and could have occupied the vacancies created by the evil angels in heaven. That was not to be because of the entrance of sin. Nevertheless, God did not abandon the project. It is only momentarily delayed because He is in the process of dealing with sin, and after it all, those who will overcome will be admitted into the heavens above to have the status of angels.

Knowing that God's aim for a couple is to procreate, it follows that God did not create individuals to be single. Singleness is not God's idea, and the church should not encourage or promote it. This is because God, in His wisdom, has created a man and a woman with a wiring system that makes it difficult for them to live separate lives without being married. If we want to live to please God, then we have to follow His plan, for it leads us to salvation. But if we just want to live to please the devil, then we can choose to live outside God's plan. When we choose to live outside God's plan, it means we are taking the side of the devil in the great controversy.

Singleness is a result of sin. Some people, especially single people, will be angry at this point, but it is very true. There are different types of single people, and I would like to demonstrate that it is all because of sin.

- Widows: A man or a woman becomes single due to the death of his/her partner. We all know that death is a result of sin. It is because of sin that we have many widows in our churches and the society at large. No one can choose to be single through the death of a partner.
- Divorcees: When a marriage breaks apart, the partners choose to live separately as singles. God hates divorce, and divorce is a result of sin. No one wants to divorce once they are married. This is a direct result of the devil wreaking havoc in our marriages.
- Separation: When people are not married, they are not recognised before God as a couple. Because of sin,

some people get involved in relationships that meet their immediate needs. Because of sexual needs, young people engage in sex before marriage. Some people just agree to live together without being married. When such a relationship breaks apart, I do not call it a divorce, for it was not a marriage in the first place. I call it separation. Whatever the relationship was, there is bound to be some disappointment, and as a result of that separation, some people choose to remain single.

- Physical Defects: There are some people who think that Paul chose to be single, but from the epistle quoted above, it does not seem so. Paul says that he wished every man was like him, but since there were differences between Paul and other men, he encouraged them and permitted them to marry lest they sin against God. Some commentators suggest that Paul had a certain physical condition that made it impossible for him to marry. These conditions, although not common, are also present in our society. Some people are born with a condition that does not allow them to marry. Some people develop these conditions because of certain types of diseases. While we agree that this is very unfortunate, we should also agree that this is a result of sin. It is not God who created all these unfortunate circumstances. It is the devil.
- Rejection: There is a certain singleness that is created by rejection. There are certain people who wish to be married, but they just cannot find someone who wants to marry them. Although this is not common, it is there. Again, it is not one's choice but a direct result of the devil's plan to frustrate the plan of God in humanity.

- Choice: Some people are single by choice. I would not like to dwell much on this topic because it is not biblical. One can choose to be single outside the biblical context, but within the context of the Bible, there is no such thing. The verse is clear, "It is not good for a man to be alone." This statement is from God Himself. I do not think there is any bible-believing Christian who will one day wake up in his rightful senses and declare, "It is good for a man to be alone." This is the direct opposite of the word of God, and it is inspired by the devil.

I have tried to prove without any reasonable doubt that singleness is a result of sin. Therefore, the church should deal with singles the way Christ would deal with anyone. When I say singleness is a result of sin, it does not follow that the one who is single is a sinner. It means that the condition is a product of the devil who has come to steal joy and happiness from God's families. There is one major reason why God cannot allow a person to live a single life: it is adultery. The sin of adultery is rampant in the world that we are living in. In some quarters of our society, adultery is practised to such an extent that even Christians no longer consider adultery as sinful as God does.

Paul emphasises that, because of adultery or the temptation to commit adultery, each man should have his own wife. What Paul is doing is just repeating what God said in the beginning. Since God knew the kind of wires he had put in Adam, He created Eve to meet those needs, and He declared that it was not good for Adam to live without Eve. It is not good for couples to live separately because the situation will create an environment which makes it possible for human beings to commit the sin of adultery. This is the reason why God said that once a man is married, he should leave his family and cleave to his wife. The two should not be physically separated by any circumstances in life. Couples are not allowed to live in separate places, even because of work. God-fearing couples should never even think of living separately. God wants to put a strong hedge around a marriage so that there is no room for committing adultery.

Remember, only through the sin of adultery may a couple seek to divorce, but remember also that God hates divorce. Thus, as the couple is living together, some sins, such as anger or fighting, may exist, and God, through His grace, will be working through these weaknesses, but the sin of adultery should never be allowed to penetrate a marriage. God has given us enough light to know that a person should defend himself/herself against the sin of adultery with his/her life. Perhaps on this point, we should adopt Paul's statement that we have not yet fought until blood oozes out of our bodies. The war against the sin of adultery is not a simple one. Any honest Christian will know that.

Many people would want to push the agenda of being single, successful and independent. However, these are ideas from the human rights and women's rights movements. These are not the ideas of God. It is not about getting success in the world of business or academics; it is about getting success against the sin of adultery. Many single people who advocate for that have left a trail of children behind them. The question that needs to be answered is very simple: How does a single person get children? This alone is strong evidence to support the word of God that they have failed to live alone. Many people have praised themselves for being strong, single mothers who have managed to raise their children alone. Apart from widows whose husbands have passed away, this is not an achievement. There is no crown in heaven for single mothers who have raised their children alone. The reason is very simple. Those children have a father, and together, the parents should raise their children. That's why some people become frustrated when the children they raised alone begin to look for their father or their mother when they are grown up. Statistics have shown that children who are raised by single parents undergo more emotional stress than those who are raised by both parents. Some of them will become misfits in society. Were it not for the grace of God, most of them could be lost in the world of bitterness and sorrow.

Often, people create conditions for them to be single. What do I mean? People engage themselves in pre-marital sex and become involved in a relationship with partners who are not of their faith. Some have children outside of marriage, and some even get sexually transmitted diseases before getting married. These conditions result in a weak marriage foundation. Often, these marriages do not last, creating singles in the church and society. But the question that begs to be answered will remain the same: Now that you are single, can you live a single life like Paul? Have you overcome the sin of adultery? This is a million-dollar question, and it will remain unanswered. Therefore, in our churches, there is rampant adultery to such an extent that preachers are no longer pointing at this sin. In many churches, preachers have stopped preaching about morality issues and righteousness; they only preach about prosperity. How does a church ignore a key question such as adultery in its congregation?

Because of how serious the sin of adultery is, Paul went on to encourage young widows to marry. We know that these people have lost their spouses through death, and obviously, it is not their choice, but this will not remove the fact that they still need partners to fulfil their desires, including sexual desires. Paul urges young widows to marry. Actually, Paul gives a condition on which the church should classify widows. A widow should be regarded as one if she is sixty years and above and has been living according to the light she has received from the Lord. The sin of adultery is so serious that all our young singles in church should seek to get married.

By the same token, young divorcees should also seek to marry. But, according to the Bible, this is very tricky. The Bible says God hates divorce, and people should divorce only in the case of adultery. If you are divorced because of other reasons, the Bible does not recognise that you are divorced. Any marriage that you enter thereafter is adulterous. The church cannot involve itself in adulterous marriage. However, if one is divorced because of adultery in the marriage, and you are not the guilty party, you can marry. This is so to shield one from the temptation of adultery. In the Bible, there are only two ways: Those who believe they cannot marry for any reason should live for God and live like Paul. They should read about the life of Paul after his conversion and should decide whether they can lead such a life. These should be very few. Those who advocate singleness have passions like any other human being, and to avoid burning, they should marry.

7| Polygamy Is a Distortion of God's Image of Marriage

Genesis 1:26 – *And God said, "Let us make man in our image, after our likeness: and let them have dominion over the fish of the sea, and over the fowl of the air, and over the cattle, and over all the earth, and over every creeping thing that creepeth upon the earth."*

1:27 – *So God created man in his own image, in the image of God created he him; male and female created he them.*

Malachi 2:15 – *And did not he make one? Yet had he the residue of the spirit. And wherefore one? That he might seek a godly seed. Therefore, take heed to your spirit, and let none deal treacherously against the wife of his youth.*

Genesis 4:18 – *And unto Enoch was born Irad: and Irad begat Mehujael: and Mehujael begat Methusael: and Methusael begat Lamech.*

4:19 – *And Lamech took unto him two wives: the name of the one was Adah, and the name of the other Zillah.*

4:20 – *And Adah bare Jabal: he was the father of such as dwell in tents, and of such as have cattle.*

4:21 – *And his brother's name was Jubal: he was the father of all, such as handle the harp and organ.*

4:22 – *And Zillah, she also bare Tubalcain, an instructor of every artificer in brass and iron: and the sister of Tubalcain was Naamah.*

4:23 – *And Lamech said unto his wives, "Adah and Zillah, hear my voice; ye wives of Lamech, hearken unto my speech: for I have slain a man to my wounding, and a young man to my hurt."*

4:24 – *If Cain shall be avenged sevenfold, truly Lamech seventy and sevenfold.*

11:3 – *And he had seven hundred wives, princesses, and three hundred concubines: and his wives turned away his heart.*
1 Kings 11:4 – *For it came to pass when Solomon was old that his wives turned away his heart after other gods: and his heart was not perfect with the LORD, his God, as was the heart of David, his father.*
11:5 – *For Solomon went after Ashtoreth, the goddess of the Zidonians, and after Milcom, the abomination of the Ammonites.*
11:6 – *And Solomon did evil in the sight of the LORD, and went not fully after the LORD, as did David, his father.*
11:7 – *Then did Solomon build an high place for Chemosh, the abomination of Moab, in the hill that is before Jerusalem, and for Molech, the abomination of the children of Ammon.*
11:8 – *And likewise did he for all his strange wives, which burnt incense and sacrificed unto their gods.*
11:9 – *And the LORD was angry with Solomon because his heart was turned from the LORD God of Israel, which had appeared unto him twice.*

2 Samuel

11:2 – *And it came to pass in an evening tide, that David arose from off his bed, and walked upon the roof of the king's house: and from the roof, he saw a woman washing herself; and the woman was very beautiful to look upon.*
11:3 – *And David sent and inquired after the woman. And one said, "Is not this Bathsheba, the daughter of Eliam, the wife of Uriah, the Hittite?"*
11:4 – *And David sent messengers, and took her; and she came in unto him, and he lay with her; for she was purified from her uncleanness: and she returned unto her house.*
11:5 – *And the woman conceived, and sent and told David, and said, "I am with child."*

2 Samuel

13:11 – *And when she had brought them unto him to eat, he took hold of her and said unto her, "Come lie with me, my sister."*

13:12 – *And she answered him, "Nay, my brother, do not force me; for no such thing ought to be done in Israel: do not thou this folly.*

13:13 – *And I, whither shall I cause my shame to go? And as for thee, thou shalt be as one of the fools in Israel. Now, therefore, I pray thee, speak unto the king, for he will not withhold me from thee."*

13:14 – *Howbeit he would not hearken unto her voice: but, being stronger than she, forced her, and lay with her.*

2 Samuel

13:29 – *And the servants of Absalom did unto Amnon as Absalom had commanded. Then all the king's sons arose, and every man gat him up upon his mule and fled.*

13:30 – *And it came to pass, while they were in the way, that tidings came to David, saying, "Absalom hath slain all the king's sons, and there is not one of them left."*

13:31 – *Then the king arose, and tare his garments, and lay on the earth; and all his servants stood by with their clothes rent.*

2 Samuel

20:3 – *And David came to his house at Jerusalem; and the king took the ten women his concubines, whom he had left to keep the house, and put them in ward, and fed them, but went not in unto them. So they were shut up unto the day of their death, living in widowhood.*

Genesis 16:1 – *Now, Sarai, Abram's wife, bare him no children: and she had an handmaid, an Egyptian, whose name was Hagar.*

16:2 – *And Sarai said unto Abram, "Behold now, the LORD hath restrained me from bearing: I pray thee, go in unto my maid; it may be that I may obtain children by her." And Abram hearkened to the voice of Sarai.*

16:3 – *And Sarai, Abram's wife, took Hagar, her maid, the Egyptian, after Abram had dwelt ten years in the land of Canaan, and gave her to her husband Abram to be his wife.*
16:4 – *And he went in unto Hagar, and she conceived: and when she saw that she had conceived, her mistress was despised in her eyes.*

God created one wife for Adam. Despite the fact that He had more residue of spirit to create another wife for Adam, God, in His wisdom, created only one. In the couple, God imprinted His image. As they relate to each other and other people, the couple must bear in mind that they are created in the image of God. The image of God was not complete in Adam; hence, He created Eve so that His image could be reflected. This is echoed by the book of Malachi, which gives a reason why God created only one wife for Adam. The reason is that He was seeking a Godly seed. Therefore, it follows that a polygamous marriage cannot reflect the image of God. The other point is that a polygamous family cannot produce a Godly family. From the beginning, God did not create or allow a marriage to have more than one wife. Therefore, polygamy is a sin.

The history of the beginning of polygamy can be traced from the book of Genesis. It started from the family tree of Cain, the murderer who had been chased away from the face of God. From the family of Cain, we can trace it down until we come to the man named Lameck. The man Lameck is the one who married two wives. Polygamy was started by people who had chosen to fight against God. The whole family tree of Cain was separated from the seed of Seth, the servant of God. The very people who started polygamy will reflect how ungodly the practice is. Nevertheless, the sons of God intermarried with these ungodly people and evil was found all over the face of the earth until God decided to wipe out everyone except Noah, who was a descendant of Seth and had lived according to the word of God.

In the very family of Lameck, one can notice the fighting and strife that existed from the way Lameck talked to his wives. We can also trace the existence of murder in this family because Lameck told his wife that he had slain a young man to his wounding. But the word of God continues to make a startling comment. It says that if Cain is to be avenged seven times (obviously for killing Abel), then Lameck should be avenged seventy times (for polygamy). The Bible is giving a glimpse of the picture of how bad polygamy is. The Bible is saying that polygamy is ten times as bad as murder. Difficult as it may be to understand, but it is still true. There are many people who have lived in a polygamous family and who can testify to that fact. To understand how sinful polygamy is, let us take a closer look at the lives of the patriarchs.

- **David**

God, throughout the Old Testament, points to the fact that David is His friend. David learned to trust God while he was a shepherd boy. From then on, God picked David to be the king and leader of His people. God loved David to such an extent that Jesus, in His human form, was called the son of David. Yet David's life was marred with sinful episodes that are very difficult to comprehend. The most prominent one involves the wife of Uriah, the Hittite. It should be noted that David was already married and did not need another wife. In fact, by this time, he already had other wives. The way he got the wife of Uriah is very striking. It was because of uncontrolled appetite and passion that David decided to sleep with the wife of Uriah. It was intemperance. It was covetousness. David saw the woman from the top of the roof and decided that he was going to sleep with her. As a king, he used all the resources that he had and slept with Bathsheba. From then on, since he had satisfied his sexual desires, he had nothing to do with this woman. He even called Uriah to come back from the war to sleep with his wife so that David could cover the pregnancy Bathsheba had just reported to him. The God-fearing man Uriah declined to sleep in his house as long as other soldiers were at war, so David decided to kill him.

People who marry many wives have no reason for doing that except the reasons that were cited as to why David took Uriah's wife. It is covetousness. It is uncontrolled appetite and passion. It is gross intemperance. It is a sin at its worst, and such people do not inherit the kingdom of God unless they repent, just as David did, as we shall see shortly. From coveting Uriah's wife, David went on to kill her husband. It is now clear that those who have many wives are ten times worse than murderers, for the underlying spirit is that of a murderer. Because of his polygamous family, from then on, David did not please God. His family was full of atrocities that God allowed to be penned only for our admonition. The son of David, Amnon, from another mother, raped his sister, Tamar, from the mother of Absolom. These brothers were enemies from then until Absalom got the chance to kill Amnon. Absalom went on to turn against his father's kingdom and led a rebel group to fight against David's kingdom. Because of the sin of polygamy, David did not see peace in his last days on the earth. David passed through anguish of soul and witnessed numerous murderers because of his having taken many wives. Only God knows the souls that were lost eternally because of this family set-up. David also passed this legacy on to his sons, especially, as we shall see, in the life of Solomon.

However, David did not end his life in a polygamous family. He repented. First of all, it is imperative to note that David repented for the sin of taking Bathsheba and killing Uriah. His prayer of confession, especially regarding this matter, is found in Psalms 51. Secondly, it is also important to note that David repented for the sin of polygamy. He took all the ten concubines, gave them shelter and food and did not sleep with them again. There are some people who are in polygamy and want to know what they must do. The answer is very simple: They must follow David's path. They must realise that the Bible does not recognise the second wife, or third and so on, as a wife. The Bible calls them concubines. Sleeping with them is adultery and is a sin before God. They should repent for this and never sleep with these women for the rest of their lives. They should only sleep with their first wife, who is the legitimate wife according to the Bible. However, David did not just turn his back on these people. He also provided shelter and food for these women and maintained them. The issue of maintenance did not start in the 21st century. Christians should know that it is their duty to maintain the children that they have outside their legitimate family. It is a lifetime responsibility that one has to take. God-fearing people should not wait for the courts of this land to force them to pay maintenance for the concubines and the children they have outside the legitimate marriage. These people are their responsibility.

- **Solomon**

Among the people who have lived on this planet, there is no one wiser than Solomon. People flocked from all corners of the earth to see King Solomon. Surprisingly, Solomon was the child of David and Bathsheba (Uriah's wife). God loved and favoured King Solomon. He was rich and had access to whatever his heart desired. In his early days, King Solomon lived to please God. Solomon built a magnificent temple for the Lord in Jerusalem. He judged his people with wisdom, and his people loved him. All this came to an end when Solomon married many wives. The beautiful life of King Solomon was tainted in his later years by his love for foreign women. Instead of marrying one God-fearing wife, Solomon married strange women from places other than Judah or Israel. The Bible records a bitter end to Solomon's life. Because of the women he married, he went after worshipping other gods. He even erected high places for these gods. This was strange for a man who built a magnificent temple for the Lord. During the dedication of the temple, Solomon prayed and prayed until the holy Shekinah appeared in the temple. This signified the presence of God Himself. This is the same Solomon who started to worship the gods of Ashtoreth and Molech and erected high places for them. Solomon forgot the Lord God of Israel, who endowed him with wisdom. All this was only because of polygamy. By now, we should understand why polygamy is worse than committing murder.

Solomon's life, according to the Book of Kings, did not end well. The Bible says that the Lord God of Israel was angry with Solomon. I still harbour the belief that Solomon will not be there in heaven because of how the book of 1 Kings ends the life history of Solomon. However, the pen of inspiration traces that Solomon wrote the books of Ecclesiastes when he was repenting, and from this point alone, we shall see Solomon in heaven. However, the story of Solomon was written for our admonition. People who follow the lifestyle of Solomon in relation to his married life will find it difficult to come back to their Creator and are at the risk of losing eternal life.

❖ Abraham

I also trace the life of Abraham, the father of faith. Abraham was chosen by God himself and was promised a child. Abraham failed to wait for the promised child and devised his own means to have a child. It was a grave mistake. Through his wife Sarah, he decided to take Hagar, Sarah's servant, as a wife. The moment Hagar conceived a child, Abraham's family had no peace. There was jealousy, strife, bigotry and many wars between Sarah and Hagar. Certainly, this was not what Abraham hoped for. This was not expected from the family of the man of God's choice. Abraham's family was supposed to reflect the image of God, not the image of the devil. Abraham's sin of polygamy not only disturbed his immediate family alone, but the effects are still felt even in our generation. Hagar gave birth to a son named Ishmael. Ishmael is the father of present-day Muslims. When God's time had come, and He fulfilled the promise of giving Abraham the promised child, Sarah gave birth to Isaac. Isaac is the father of present-day Jews. Since the days of Abraham, there has been no peace in the Middle East because of these two nations from the two sons of Abraham from two different mothers. Only eternity can estimate the souls that were lost eternally due to the wars in the Middle East. All this happened only because of one man who decided to move away from the promise of God and marry two wives. People continue to underestimate the negative impact that polygamy will bring to the lives of people.

- **Jacob**

Jacob ended up in an unfortunate situation where he had to marry four wives: two sisters, Leah and Rachel and their respective maidservants. The family of Jacob was marked by unhappiness. There was competition and jealousy. Jacob did not help the situation because the Bible says he loved Rachel more than Leah. This favouritism was also prominent with his children. Jacob loved Joseph and Benjamin because they were the sons of the wife he loved most, Rachel. This prompted the elder brothers to hate Joseph. They hated Joseph so much that they wanted to kill him. Had it not been for the intervention of one of the brothers, Joseph could have been killed. They, however, decided to sell Joseph and reported to their father that Joseph had been killed by wild animals. This was not easy for Jacob. For the rest of his life, he thought he had lost his son. Though the story ended with a reunion, the suffering which was brought upon this family was unmistakably revealed. There are many polygamous situations in the Bible and outside the Bible that I have not mentioned. Why did the Bible record all these sad stories? So that the people of God can learn how sinful adultery and polygamy is and can shun it. The results of polygamy are devastating, destructive and long-lasting. Those who desire to worship the God who instituted marriage must shun polygamy. Polygamy destroys the image of God in marriage and produces ungodly families. It predisposes families to be defeated by the devil rather than to defeat him. Many souls will be eternally lost because of problems associated with adultery and polygamy.

8| Ordination of Women Is Impossible with God

Ephesians
5:22 – *Wives, submit yourselves unto your own husbands, as unto the Lord.*
5:23 – *For the husband is the head of the wife, even as Christ is the head of the church: and he is the saviour of the body.*
5:24 – *Therefore as the church is subject unto Christ, so let the wives be to their own husbands in everything.*
1 Timothy
3:1 – *This is a true saying, "If a man desires the office of a bishop, he desireth a good work."*
3:2 – *A bishop then must be blameless, the husband of one wife, vigilant, sober, of good behaviour, given to hospitality, apt to teach;*
3:3 – *Not given to wine, no striker, not greedy of filthy lucre; but patient, not a brawler, not covetous;*
3:4 *One that ruleth well his own house, having his children in subjection with all gravity;*
3:5 – *(For if a man know not how to rule his own house, how shall he take care of the church of God?)*
Titus 1:5 – *For this cause left I thee in Crete that thou shouldest set in order the things that are wanting, and ordain elders in every city, as I had appointed thee:*
1:6 – *If any be blameless, the husband of one wife, having faithful children not accused of riot or unruly.*
1:7 – *For a bishop must be blameless, as the steward of God; not self-willed, not soon angry, not given to wine, no striker, not given to filthy lucre;*
1:8 – *But a lover of hospitality, a lover of good men, sober, just, holy, temperate;*

1:9 – *Holding fast the faithful word as he hath been taught, that he may be able by sound doctrine both to exhort and to convince the gainsayers.*

Acts 6:3 – *Wherefore, brethren, look ye out among you seven men of honest report, full of the Holy Ghost and wisdom, whom we may appoint over this business.*

6:4 – *But we will give ourselves continually to prayer, and to the ministry of the word.*

6:5 – *And the saying pleased the whole multitude: and they chose Stephen, a man full of faith and of the Holy Ghost, and Philip, and Prochorus, and Nicanor, and Timon, and Parmenas, and Nicolas, a proselyte of Antioch:*

6:6 – *Whom they set before the apostles: and when they had prayed, they laid their hands on them.*

1 Timothy

3:8 – *Likewise must the deacons be grave, not double-tongued, not given to much wine, not greedy of filthy lucre;*

3:9 – *Holding the mystery of the faith in a pure conscience.*

3:10 – *And let these also first be proved; then let them use the office of a deacon, being found blameless.*

3:11 – *Even so must their wives be grave, not slanderers, sober, faithful in all things.*

3:12 – *Let the deacons be the husbands of one wife, ruling their children and their own houses well.*

3:13 – *For they that have used the office of a deacon well purchase to themselves a good degree, and great boldness in the faith which is in Christ Jesus.*

1 Corinthians

14:34 – *Let your women keep silence in the churches: for it is not permitted unto them to speak; but they are commanded to be under obedience, as also saith the law.*

14:35 – *And if they will learn anything, let them ask their husbands at home: for it is a shame for women to speak in the church.*

Revelation

19:7 – *Let us be glad and rejoice, and give honour to him: for the marriage of the Lamb is come, and his wife hath made herself ready.*

19:8 – *And to her was granted that she should be arrayed in fine linen, clean and white: for the fine linen is the righteousness of saints.*

19:9 – *And he saith unto me, "Write, blessed are they which are called unto the marriage supper of the Lamb." And he saith unto me, "These are the true sayings of God."*

The term 'ordination' and what it stands for can have different meanings depending on how it is used. For example, one can say the Lord has ordained him/her from his/her mother's womb to work for Him. I personally do not see any problem using the word 'ordination' in that way, but I want to discuss the term 'ordination' in relation to church leadership. In the Bible, there are two incidences and two specific groups of people that were ordained for church leadership positions. The first and most common is the ordination of the deacons in the Book of Acts. The seven deacons were selected and ordained for service in the early church. What is of particular importance to note is the criteria that were used to select these deacons. The following characteristics are mentioned in the Book of Acts:

- They have to be men
- They must have a good report
- They must be full of Holy Ghost
- They must be blameless
- They must hold the mystery of the faith in a pure conscience
- They must be husbands of one wife
- They must rule their children well

The other group of people who were ordained in the Bible were elders. Paul gave instruction to Titus to ordain elders in every city. It is also critical that I list the characteristics of the elders as mentioned in the Bible, and it is important to mention that the word 'elder' in the Bible is synonymous with bishop and pastor. All three words mean the same thing, and they refer to the same office and can be used interchangeably. The criteria for choosing an elder to lead the church are as follows:

- Must be a man
- Blameless
- A husband of one wife
- Able to teach doctrine
- Sober, vigilant and of good behaviour
- Hospitable
- Not given to wine, no striker, not greedy of filthy lucre; but patient, not a brawler, not covetous;
- Rules his own house well, having his children in subjection with all gravity; (If a man knows not how to rule his own house, how shall he take care of the church of God?)

Another group of people who were ordained for leadership purposes were apostles. Apostles are different from elders. Apostles are evangelists who are not stationed in a local church. They move from place to place, especially in un-entered areas, preaching the gospel and planting churches. After the churches are planted, elders are then elected and ordained to be resident ministers in the local church. The elders and deacons will then be responsible for the running and expansion of the local church. Apostles who were ordained for the work of evangelists were the twelve apostles and, thereafter, Paul and Barnabas, and others.

In the meantime, I want to discuss the term 'ordination' in connection with the office of an elder, or bishop or pastor. This is an important office at the local church level. The office of the elder becomes the office of the head of the local church. Using the word 'leader' is sometimes misleading, depending on how we interpret it. Anyone can be a leader of some sort. My wife is the leader of my children. We have leaders in the church in various departments, such as women's ministries, family ministries, and so on. These leading positions can be occupied by anyone in the church, regardless of gender. These positions also need not have ordination. These leaders in these departments are, therefore, advisory rather than administrative. For the purposes of this discourse, I will refer to the position of the elder as the head of the church rather than the leader just to distinguish it from the ones that I have mentioned above.

Can a woman be elected to head the church and be ordained for such an office? The word of God is so clear that there is no need to discuss the topic. However, since the topic has become so critical in our churches, I find it imperative to discuss it. The reason why there is so much confusion on such a clear topic is that the devil is fighting marriage with all his powers.

How can I mention that the devil is fighting marriage when the topic under consideration is women's ordination? It is so because the relationship between a husband and a wife is an image of the relationship between Christ and His church. God is so particular about order that any disorientation of this order is a rebellion against His government. In the book of Ephesians, Paul commands women to be submissive to their husbands as unto the Lord, for the head of the woman is the man, as Christ is the head of the church. There is a parallel that cannot be ignored there. The husband's position in the home is clear and has been discussed in the previous chapters. Adam was created to be the head of the first family in the Garden of Eden, which happened to be the first church on the earth. The position of Adam as the head of both the first family and the first church cannot be disputed. God, in

His wisdom, created it that way. It was created that way before the entrance of sin into the Garden of Eden and was reemphasized after the entrance of sin into the Garden of Eden. Adam was also made the spiritual head of the first family and the first church based on the fact that the law was committed to Adam by God in the Garden of Eden. That is why one of the criteria for occupying an elder's position is the ability to teach doctrine. The doctrine of God was committed to Adam, and it is Adam who must defend the purity of the doctrine both in the home and in the church.

The other parallel between marriage and the church is the fact that the elder should be a man of one wife. The Bible is gender specific and clear about the fact that the office of the elder is for men. This point is very clear, even in this 21st century, where some of the scriptures that refer to men are being altered to language that is inclusive in light of women's rights and empowerment. However, it should be noted that no human right can change the word of God because no human right was consulted when it was written in the first place. The point that I want to dwell on is that the elder should be a man with only one wife. The elder of the church should be a man with one wife in marriage. There it is: marriage and church cannot be separated. This is because, as we have noticed in earlier chapters, a man is a representative of Christ in the home, while a woman is a representative of the church. When God instructs women to be submissive to their own husbands, He teaches a lesson about the attitude of the church towards Christ, who died for it. When Christ commands men to love their wives as Christ loves the church, He reminds the family of His love every day. Thus, the gospel of salvation is the theme of marriage and the church. We already know that themes with salvific connotations need not be confused in the Bible. They are a matter of life and death. If the husband is to be the head of the marriage and the church, it should remain so. Any interchange of the roles will result in the catastrophe of sin, just like in the Garden of Eden. As the church can never take the position of Christ, women can never take the position of men in our churches and homes. If any woman tries to do so, it may result in the distortion of the image of God both in the home and the church. Women must never be ordained to the position of elders, for this signifies the uplifting of the church to the position of Christ, which makes the church Babylon.

An elder should be a man with one wife. I do not know how the church can mistake this to mean a woman with one husband. Certainly, there is no need for such an error. It is uncalled for. It is a clear violence against the word of God, which is so plain. It is important again to see the parallel between marriage and the church in the statement. A man should have one wife because Christ has one church on earth. Christ is preparing to take one church to heaven when He comes for the second time. Christ is represented here as the husband, and the wife is the spotless church that should be ready to meet her husband. The image of Christ and the church as represented in the marriage will not end here and now; it will perpetuate in the marriage supper of the lamb, and the union will be for eternity. In matters that preach such great themes of salvation, the church need not err.

The church elder should be a man who rules his house well. He should also have his children obedient and in subjection to the Lord Jesus. Ruling the house well includes instilling God's creation order in the family and teaching the commandments of God in the family. This can be seen in the fruits of the children who will follow Christ. It is not only teaching the word of God in the family that will produce such children but also doing the word. An elder should be holy, temperate and blameless before God. He should be a representative of Christ in the marriage. The character of

Jesus should be fully reproduced in the man of God, and he should take up his God-given responsibility to lead his family and the church family in meeting Jesus. The fruits of a holy man who teaches his family the word of God are obedient children. This is a promise from God. A man who has failed to rule his own house and produce Godly children should not be given the responsibility to lead the church. He has demonstrated that he cannot stand on the position of Christ in the small family duties and cannot be trusted with similar duties of a bigger magnitude.

In all this, the wife is there, taking responsibility as the suitable helper. In the marriage, the wife is to take on her duties, particularly in raising Godly children, as the husband reaches out to the larger church family. The mother should zero in on her children before she reaches out for further fields. Since the mother's primary purpose is the children, if a mother, under the leadership of the father, fails to take care of her children properly, it means that the father has failed to be the head of the wife. Therefore, it is concluded that ruling one's household well includes effective functioning and management of family roles and responsibilities. A wife who is not effective in her duties is the result of a man who is not a representative of Jesus in that home and is, therefore, an ineffective head.

Church leadership is not the domain of the mother, and Paul instructs women to keep quiet in church. Although this instruction was not universal, it shows the universality of the fact that women need to occupy positions in the church that show humility and submissiveness to men. In terms of doctrine and leadership, women should never occupy those positions that suggest that they have authority over men. This is a biblical instruction from creation, and it should be adhered to. A church that is not in line with the organogram of God (God the Father – Christ – husband – wife – children) is a misrepresentation of God. In line with God's plan, the office of the apostle, elder (bishop or pastor) and deacons should be reserved for the male gender.

There can be no mistake on this point from scripture. These offices require that those elected to occupy them should be ordained by the laying of hands. It follows that the ordination of women to any of the above offices is unbiblical. No other offices except the above ones are designated by the Bible to require ordination. It also follows that the ordination of women in general is unbiblical. Our wives, mothers and sisters are free to work for the Lord using their spiritual gifts and can also occupy any leadership position in the church and home other than the ones discussed above, including those that may insinuate that they have authority over men.

9| Adultery Is More Than a Sin

Romans 3:23 – *For all have sinned, and come short of the glory of God;*

John 3:16 – *For God so loved the world, that he gave his only begotten Son, that whosoever believeth in him should not perish, but have everlasting life.*

Genesis 1:27 – *So God created man in his own image, in the image of God created he him; male and female created he them.*

Deuteronomy

22:13 – *If any man take a wife, and go in unto her, and hate her,*

22:14 – *And give occasions of speech against her, and bring up an evil name upon her, and say, "I took this woman, and when I came to her, I found her, not a maid:"*

22:15 – *Then shall the father of the damsel, and her mother take and bring forth the tokens of the damsel's virginity unto the elders of the city in the gate:*

22:16 – *And the damsel's father shall say unto the elders, "I gave my daughter unto this man to wife, and he hateth her;*

22:17 – *And, lo, he hath given occasions of speech against her, saying, 'I found not thy daughter a maid;' and yet these are the tokens of my daughter's virginity." And they shall spread the cloth before the elders of the city.*

22:18 – *And the elders of that city shall take that man and chastise him;*

22:19 – *And they shall amerce him in an hundred shekels of silver, and give them unto the father of the damsel because he hath brought up an evil name upon a virgin of Israel: and she shall be his wife; he may not put her away all his days.*

22:20 – *But if this thing be true, and the tokens of virginity be not found for the damsel:*

22:21 – *Then they shall bring out the damsel to the door of her father's house, and the men of her city shall stone her with stones that she die: because she hath wrought folly in Israel, to play the whore in her father's house: so shalt thou put evil away from among you.*

22:22 – *If a man be found lying with a woman married to an husband, then they both shall die, both the man that lay with the woman and the woman: so shalt thou put away evil from Israel.*

22:23 – *If a damsel that is a virgin be betrothed unto an husband, and a man find her in the city, and lie with her;*

22:24 – *Then ye shall bring them both out unto the gate of that city, and ye shall stone them with stones that they die; the damsel, because she cried not, being in the city; and the man, because he hath humbled his neighbour's wife: so thou shalt put away evil from among you.*

22:25 – *But if a man find a betrothed damsel in the field, and the man force her, and lie with her: then the man only that lay with her shall die:*

22:26 – *But unto the damsel thou shalt do nothing; there is in the damsel no sin worthy of death: for as when a man riseth against his neighbour, and slayeth him, even so is this matter:*

22:27 – *For he found her in the field, and the betrothed damsel cried, and there was none to save her.*

22:28 – *If a man find a damsel that is a virgin, which is not betrothed, and lay hold on her, and lie with her, and they be found;*

22:29 – *Then the man that lay with her shall give unto the damsel's father fifty shekels of silver, and she shall be his wife; because he hath humbled her, he may not put her away all his days.*

Hebrews

13:4 – *Marriage is honourable in all, and the bed undefiled: but whoremongers and adulterers God will judge.*

1 Corinthians
6:15 – *Know ye not that your bodies are the members of Christ? Shall I then take the members of Christ, and make them the members of an harlot? God forbid.*
6:16 – *What? Know ye not that he which is joined to an harlot is one body for two, saith he, shall be one flesh?*
6:17 – *But he that is joined unto the Lord is one spirit.*
6:18 – *Flee fornication. Every sin that a man doeth is without the body; but he that committeth fornication sinneth against his own body.*
6:19 – *What? Know ye not that your body is the temple of the Holy Ghost which is in you, which ye have of God, and ye are not your own?*
6:20 – *For ye are bought with a price: therefore glorify God in your body, and in your spirit, which are God's.*
Exodus 20:14 – *Thou shalt not commit adultery.*

All human beings have sinned and have fallen short of the glory of God. It means that after God created humanity in His image, Adam and Eve fell into sin by choosing to disobey God. The image of God in them was marred by the presence of sin. Thereafter, all descendants of Adam and Eve inherited the sinful nature and its consequences. Anyone born on the earth has the propensity to sin and has guaranteed death. After the entrance of sin into the Garden of Eden, God did not leave the human race to perish in their sinful nature. God sent His only begotten son so that whoever believes in Him will not perish but have eternal life. In Jesus, humanity not only guaranteed its victory over sin but also restored the image of God and inherited eternal life.

This should especially be understood in the context of marriage. This is so because the image of God was created in the male and female. The first mention of the creation of man in the image of God was the creation of the image of the male and female. The image of God in humanity should especially be understood in the marriage set up. The Bible reiterates that when two people, male and female, are joined together in the institution of marriage, they become one. Paul further explains that the oneness is cemented by the act of sex. In this context, the marriage becomes the image of God. God is one, but there are three co-eternal persons in this one God. In marriage, we have two distinct individuals, but when they come together in the holy institution of marriage and commit themselves to procreate through the gift of sex, they become one. They begin to share blood through sex, and their offspring share the blood of both; they become one.

For this reason, the sin of adultery should be dreaded by all Christians. Remember, through marriage, God is in the business of restoring His image in humanity. The image was marred by the presence of sin in human beings, but God did not leave His people to suffer eternal death. Through Christ, He is busy restoring His image in humanity. The sin of adultery especially hinders this work. In the first place, the Bible does not allow any sexual acts between people who are not married. That is called fornication.

Fornication is strictly prohibited in the Bible. God gives a clear picture of how to deal with fornicators. Any young man and young woman who sleep together are not allowed to separate themselves anymore. They engage in an act that binds them together. Since they commit a sin, they should seek to repent for their sin and regularise their relationship through marriage. God has been very strict on the issue of virginity, as is pointed out in the book of Deuteronomy. The reason why the subject of virginity is so crucial is the fact that whosoever you sleep with for the first time should be regarded as your husband or your wife. That is why, when one of the partners pretends to be a virgin, and it is discovered later, after all the marriage rights are performed, that it is not so, the pretender is to be put to death. There was no room for sex before marriage in the laws that God gave to Israel.

Because of the presence of sin in humanity, the sin of fornication existed in the church of Israel, but God gave instructions to deal with it severely. Rape and abuse were strictly forbidden as well. All offenders were punished by death. The example of how the children of the patriarch Jacob's sons dealt with the Shechemites when they raped their sister Dinah reveals how much the sin of rape was hated in Israel. After their sister was raped, the children of Israel killed all the men of Shechem. That was a horrific massacre that took place only because one Israelite girl was raped. The Bible addresses all matters that we might need to deal with regarding the topic of abuse and rape. There is no need to turn to human rights pressure groups and women empowerment groups like POWA as if our God is silent on the matter. Fornication is a sin that God hates because it places the marriage on a shaky foundation. When a marriage struggles to be intact and eventually breaks up because of a shaky foundation, the work of God in restoring the image of God in humanity is greatly hindered.

The sin of fornication is not tolerated before God. God does not tolerate any sin, but the sin of adultery and fornication will top the list if sins were to be ranked. This is so because two people who are joined together in sex become one. When people decide to join themselves outside of holy marriage, they commit an abomination. Paul explains this clearly. When a young man or woman commits fornication, that person joins himself or herself to the other person. When a person commits fornication with a whore, he becomes one with the whore. When a person commits fornication with a demon-possessed person, he or she becomes a partaker of the demons. The two become one flesh. Imagine being one flesh with a demon-possessed whore! You also become a demon-possessed whore.

Paul advises the youth to flee from the sin of fornication. Like a person who runs for his/her life when he/she meets a lion in an open forest, a young man and woman should run away from adultery. Paul also explains that other sins are better because they happen outside the body, but fornication happens right inside someone's body. It implies that when people engage in sexual activities, they share their blood. They share part of themselves. They become one. Sex becomes a blood covenant, and blood covenants are not to be broken. It is difficult for a person to stop having sex once he/she starts because it happens right inside the body. It is the chemistry that only God can explain, and when He created it, He wanted it to achieve bonding and oneness in the married couple so that they would eventually reflect the image of God. Now, due to sexual perversion and rampant adultery and fornication in this world, the bonding and oneness is happening between demons, murderers, idolaters, Satanists and so on. It will be very difficult to restore the image of God in those types of bonding, and the sin of adultery and fornication is producing devastating results, not only in the present world but also in the world to come.

Having sex outside marriage between married people or between one married partner and one single partner is the sin of adultery. Though it has the same effects as fornication, it is also devastating to married people. Apart from ravaging the souls of the partners involved, it ripples effects on the children born in this marriage and other people associated with the couple. Married people should run away from adultery. The marriage bed should be kept pure. Adultery is the worst and last thing that should ever happen in a marriage. It is hurtful; it destroys, confuses, and kills. God's commandment is very clear on this matter: *thou shall not commit adultery*. Partners who go outside of marriage to commit adultery bring demons inside the marriage. Some of the demons are very physical, such as HIV and some of the demons are spiritual. They form other bonds outside of the marriage bonds. They sell their bodies to the devil. That is why people who commit adultery continue to do so despite the pain and suffering they cause to their partners and their children. They sell their soul to the devil, and the bond becomes difficult to break.

Adultery is an abomination. It completely obliterates the image of God in a couple. It completely destroys the picture of God that He ordained from the beginning. Remember, the husband in a family is a representative of Jesus Christ, and adultery destroys the progress of the formation of Christ-like character that God intends to achieve through marriage. Remember, the wife is a representation of God's pure church. Adultery leaves a distorted picture of the work that Christ is doing for the church to such an extent that people whom God calls to His church see no reason to join the church. Through adultery, abuse and divorce, people see no image of God in a marriage. Most people rather choose to remain single or get involved in other marriage perversions. And when this happens, Satan gains an advantage. There will be, like it is now, uncontrolled sexual perversions and same-sex marriage up until the cup of iniquity of planet Earth is full. One of the factors that will push Christ to come is the extinction of matrimony and the legalization of marriage perversions such as homosexuality, lesbianism and sodomy, just like in Sodom and Gomorrah.

10| Homosexuality Is Treason

Genesis 19:1– *And there came two angels to Sodom at even; and Lot sat in the gate of Sodom: and Lot seeing them rose up to meet them; and he bowed himself with his face toward the ground;*
19:2 – *And he said, "Behold now, my lords, turn in, I pray you, into your servant's house, and tarry all night, and wash your feet, and ye shall rise up early, and go on your ways." And they said, "Nay, but we will abide in the street all night."*
19:3 – *And he pressed upon them greatly; and they turned in unto him, and entered into his house; and he made them a feast, and did bake unleavened bread, and they did eat.*
19:4 – *But before they lay down, the men of the city, even the men of Sodom, compassed the house round, both old and young, all the people from every quarter:*
19:5 – *And they called unto Lot, and said unto him, "Where are the men which came in to thee this night? Bring them out unto us, that we may know them."*
19:6 – *And Lot went out at the door unto them, and shut the door after him,*
19:7 – *And said, "I pray you, brethren, do not so wickedly.*
19:8 – *Behold now, I have two daughters which have not known man; let me, I pray you, bring them out unto you, and do ye to them as is good in your eyes: only unto these men do nothing; for therefore came they under the shadow of my roof."*
19:9 – *And they said, "Stand back." And they said again, "This one fellow came in to sojourn, and he will needs be a judge: now will we deal worse with thee, than with them." And they pressed sore upon the man, even Lot, and came near to break the door.*
19:10 – *But the men put forth their hand, pulled Lot into the house to them, and shut the door.*

19:11 – *And they smote the men that were at the door of the house with blindness, both small and great: so that they wearied themselves to find the door.*

Genesis 19:24 – *Then the LORD rained upon Sodom and upon Gomorrah brimstone and fire from the LORD out of heaven;*

19:25 – *And he overthrew those cities, and all the plain, and all the inhabitants of the cities, and that which grew upon the ground.*

Leviticus

18:22 – *Thou shalt not lie with mankind, as with womankind: it is abomination.*

Romans 1:21 – *Because that, when they knew God, they glorified him not as God, neither were thankful; but became vain in their imaginations, and their foolish heart was darkened.*

1:22 – *Professing themselves to be wise, they became fools,*

1:23 – *And changed the glory of the uncorruptible God into an image made like to corruptible man, and to birds, and four-footed beasts, and creeping things.*

1:24 – *Wherefore God also gave them up to uncleanness through the lusts of their own hearts, to dishonour their own bodies between themselves:*

1:25 – *Who changed the truth of God into a lie and worshipped and served the creature more than the Creator, who is blessed forever. Amen.*

1:26 – *For this cause God gave them up unto vile affections: for even their women did change the natural use into that which is against nature:*

1:27 – *And likewise also the men, leaving the natural use of the woman, burned in their lust one toward another; men with men working that which is unseemly, and receiving in themselves that recompense of their error which was meet.*

The Bible is very clear on the issue of homosexuality, gayism and lesbianism. It is forbidden by the Creator God. It is surprising how this topic has become a topic of intense argument among Bible-believing Christians. According to the Bible, the sin of men lying with other men or women lying with other women is called *abomination*. Abomination is a word that describes an act that is more than a sin. It is a deliberate and defiant act to fight against the government of God.

When God created marriage, it was between a man and a woman. God commanded the man and the woman to be fruitful and multiply. In other words, the man and the woman were commanded by God to procreate by using the gift that God bestowed upon them, the gift of sex. This is the ultimate objective that marriage has to fulfil in the plan of God. Apart from the union through sex between two individuals of the opposite sex, there cannot be any reproduction or procreation of any kind. Even in this scientific age, where science has gone so far as to introduce ways of reproduction, such as cloning and genetic modification, it is still proven beyond doubt that reproduction is between a male and a female.

God did not leave that to men alone. In God's other creations, reproduction is between a male and a female. In both plants and animals, God's handwriting on the will of reproduction is clear. Be fruitful and multiply. This is only possible through the mating of a male and a female of the same kind to reproduce the same species.

The idea became clear when God wanted to destroy this planet through the flood in the days of Noah. Because of wickedness, God wanted to destroy the generation of the antediluvian. But God's purpose was not to completely end the existence of life on earth. He left himself a remnant, both in the human family, through Noah's righteous family, and also in the animal kingdom. God's command in this regard was very clear. Noah was instructed to preserve animals in the ark, two by two. This was a male and a female. Noah's family was also preserved as pairs. It was Noah with his wife and then his three sons, each with his wife. Through this seed, the earth was replenished again with humanity and animal life.

It is clear that God, in His wisdom, ordained marriage for procreation through the gift of sex. There cannot be any form of sexual union that does not involve a male and a female. If it does not, then that cannot be sex. It is sexual perversion, an abomination before God. In the same manner, there cannot be any marriage apart from that of a male and a female. Anything else cannot be marriage. It is a perversion of the gift of marriage and an abomination. It is a pity that the church has departed from a clear "thus says the Lord" and has succumbed to the pressure of demons masquerading themselves as LGBT rights groups. There is no human rights group that will have a say on how marriage should be because they were not there when God created it and ordained it. As already alluded to in the introduction, marriage is the first institution that God created, blessed and sanctified (made holy). It is the image of God. Marriage represents both the oneness and order of the Godhead as they continue to work for humanity in the plan of redemption. To tamper with the only institution that reflects the image of God here on earth is not only a sin but also a crime. It is a direct insult to the government of God. Tampering with the holy institution of Jehovah, the world has triggered a wrong button that will force Jesus to rise from His throne and come back to the earth to put a stop to the nonsense called homosexuality, lesbianism and gay "marriages."

In trying to justify the existence of these abominations, these human rights groups have preached the gospel of human rights to the world. They have also resorted to falsified scientific information to try and justify that it is God who creates some people with inclinations to like partners of the same sex. They have labelled those who stand on the pillar of the word of God as people who do not care about our brothers and sisters who were created gay by God Himself. In this aspect, the world has misrepresented both God and science. First of all, any existence of gay relationships is not from the hands of God. From the hands of the Creator were male (Adam) and female (Eve). There is no other chapter in the Bible where God has created another set or order of human life. Making a male and a female, the Lord God has created and ordained the institution of marriage. It follows then that to say that any other form of marriage was created by God is a lie. It was not from God. It was from the enemy of God, the devil. It is demonic.

The Bible denies the fact that the inclination to like a partner of the same sex is a result of some genetic makeup. In the book of Romans, the apostle Paul has clearly outlined that this one is a lifestyle problem. Paul has explained that the existence of lesbians and homosexuals is a direct result of the people who have refused to listen to the word of God. It is a result of the people who have followed their own appetites and passions and their vain imaginations. It is a result of people who have refused to worship the God of heaven and have resorted to worshipping their gods of silver and gold and the gods made of metal and wood. It is a result of those people who have changed the truth of God into a lie. Since people are so defiant against God, Paul explains that God has removed His light from them and has left them with the darkness they love so much. They are kept in the darkness until they are so much darkened that their women change the natural use into that which is against nature, and likewise also the men, "leaving the natural use of the woman, burned in their lust one toward another; men with men working that which is unseemly, and receiving in themselves that recompense of their error which was meet."

It is clear, therefore, that the so-called gay marriages exist not because of genetic mutations, inheritance or some scientific explanation. There is only one explanation for its existence: SIN! The only problem is that there is no reason for the existence of sin. Sin cannot be justified. If any one reason can be found to justify the existence of sin, I will cease to be a sinner because sin will cease to be sin. That's why God, in His mercy, will be justified and be worshipped forever for coming to destroy sin at the end of time.

The creation and organization of marriage have the divine stamp, and no one can tamper around with it. Because of the existence of so much sin in the world, it might seem that all hope is lost in the marriage, but this is not to be. God, in His wisdom, is giving planet Earth the chance to repent. But if people refuse to repent and persist with their animal passions, the Lord will speak at last.

It is the same scenario that existed in the cities of Sodom and Gomorrah. People carried on with their daily businesses, just as people of this present age do. People ate, drank, married and divorced, just like these days. There was also adultery, murder and robbery in the cities. The rich also oppressed the poor. People also went to schools to acquire a good education and make a living in the future. There were also churches that debated doctrines, including that of marriage. They also had to debate about lesbianism and homosexuality, whether they were scientific, genetic or evil. Let's not forget that amidst all this, there was one family, that of Lot, that stood apart from the rest by preserving the truth of God in that wicked generation. Lot was the remnant of God in those cities. Life continued in the cities of Sodom and Gomorrah until the angels of God reported to the almighty Creator that the sin of homosexuality had reached alarming levels in those cities. Pretending to be unaware of what was happening, God sent His two angels to confirm the reports.

Upon seeing the angels, the men of Sodom wanted to sleep with them, not because the angels were females but because they clearly saw that these were men. The scripture further clarifies that Lot offered to give his virgin girls to the men of Sodom, but they refused. Men wanted to lie with other men. The people of Sodom pronounced judgement upon themselves before the Creator of heaven and earth. In these cities, they turned the marriage institution upside down. Through the laws of the government, they legalized gay marriages. From the scene portrayed by the Bible in the cities of Sodom and Gomorrah, homosexuality was legalized. It became a common practice. There was no hiding. It was accepted and done everywhere. It was noble to such an extent that one could demand and fight for it. But in legalizing homosexuality and lesbianism, the cities of Sodom and Gomorrah touched the apple of the eye of God. They revolted against the government of God Himself. Any revolt against the government is called treason, and there is only one penalty for treason: it is death. God, in His wisdom, overthrew these cities in the lake of fire. Are we, the people on planet Earth, not heading in the same direction?

11| Mirror Concept in the Marriage
Righteousness through Marriage

Genesis 1:26 – *And God said, "Let us make man in our image, after our likeness: and let them have dominion over the fish of the sea, and over the fowl of the air, and over the cattle, and over all the earth, and over every creeping thing that creepeth upon the earth."*
1:27 – *So God created man in his own image, in the image of God created he him; male and female created he them.*
1:28 – *And God blessed them, and God said unto them, "Be fruitful, and multiply, and replenish the earth, and subdue it: and have dominion over the fish of the sea, and over the fowl of the air, and over every living thing that moveth upon the earth."*
Malachi 2:15 – *And did not he make one? Yet had he the residue of the spirit. And wherefore one? That he might seek a godly seed. Therefore, take heed to your spirit, and let none deal treacherously against the wife of his youth.*
Ephesians
5:21 – *Submitting yourselves one to another in the fear of God.*
5:22 – *Wives, submit yourselves unto your own husbands, as unto the Lord.*
5:23 – *For the husband is the head of the wife, even as Christ is the head of the church: and he is the saviour of the body.*
5:24 – *Therefore, as the church is subject unto Christ, so let the wives be to their own husbands in everything.*
5:25 – *Husbands, love your wives, even as Christ also loved the church and gave himself for it;*
5:26 – *That he might sanctify and cleanse it with the washing of water by the word,*

5:27 – *That he might present it to himself a glorious church, not having spot, or wrinkle, or any such thing; but that it should be holy and without blemish.*

5:28 – *So ought men to love their wives as their own bodies. He that loveth his wife loveth himself.*

5:29 – *For no man ever yet hated his own flesh; but nourisheth and cherisheth it, even as the Lord the church:*

5:30 – *For we are members of his body, of his flesh, and of his bones.*

5:31 – *For this cause shall a man leave his father and mother, and shall be joined unto his wife, and they two shall be one flesh.*

5:32 – *This is a great mystery: but I speak concerning Christ and the church.*

An image is an exact representation of the original. The image and the original may differ in size, depending on the scale used to reproduce the image, but the bottom line is that the image is the representation of the original in all aspects. The best example of the image is when one looks at himself/herself in the mirror. The mirror reflects the image, which is exactly the same as the original except in the size in some cases.

When God created man in His own image, He envisaged that man would reflect the image of God as the mirror reflects a person's image. We should also bear in mind that the image here is not in reference to Adam but in reference to humanity. The Bible says, "So God created man in his own image, in the image of God created he him; male and female created he them." Therefore, it is clear that the image is in the "them" – male and female. For the image of God to be complete, it takes the two. It is not possible for just one individual to reflect the image of God. By grace, through the Holy Spirit, an individual can reproduce the character of Christ in himself, but no individual can reflect the image of

God. For the marriage to reflect the image of God, the couple should understand the attributes of their creator. These are the attributes that the couple should help each other to achieve. The relationship between a male and a female in a marriage should be edifying in nature, uplifting the two individuals in the likeness of Jesus and, hence, reflecting the image of God. Let us not forget that this image of God was engraved in humanity at creation, only to be marred by the entrance of sin into the human family. Therefore, marriage should exist to restore the image of God.

The couples should always remember the words of the prophet Malachi if they happen to lose the direction of their existence: "And did not he (God) make one? Yet had he the residue of the spirit. And wherefore one? That he might seek a godly seed (Reflection of the image of God). Therefore, take heed to your spirit, and let none deal treacherously against the wife of his youth." It is clear that God could have allowed many forms of marriage - such as polygamy, gay marriages and many others - but He specifically ordained one that is made up of ONE male and ONE female for Him to seek a Godly seed.

It is, therefore, conclusive that man cannot attain holiness if he shifts from the idea of God's marriage because it was specifically designed for a purpose. Humanity may try to justify all forms of relationships, but they are just trying to be another Cain, seeking salvation through their own means.

The following are the attributes of God that the marriage should seek to attain:

- Holiness (God is holy)
- Righteousness (God is righteous)
- Perfection (God is perfect)

When the Holy Spirit bears its fruit in humanity, the above attributes are inevitable. The fruit of the spirit is love, joy, peace, long-suffering, gentleness, goodness, faith, meekness and temperance.

In the marriage, the husband is the representative of Christ, while the wife is the representative of the church. When Paul was writing to the Ephesians about the relationship between a husband and a wife, he concluded by reminding his hearers that he was talking about the great mystery of Christ and His church. Therefore, one cannot talk about the husband and wife without talking about Christ and His church. The subject is not spiritual; it is carnal.

If a husband and a wife want to run their marriage to restore the image of God in humanity, they should change their attitude towards each other. If a wife regards their home as a little heaven and her husband as the representative of Jesus in that little heaven, she will change her attitude towards her husband. If a husband regards their home as a little heaven and his wife as a small church that Christ died for, he will change his attitude towards his wife. That change of attitude towards each other will be the beginning of the restoration of the image of God. Both the husband and the wife will act as a mirror to each other. The question of what role one's wife should play in their marriage will change, and vice versa. The questions that one would like their marriage to answer will also change in that respect. There will be a complete change of mindset. Questions will change from, "What should my wife do for me to show that she respects me as her husband?" to "What should I do for my wife so that I fulfil my role as the representative of Christ in this home?" There will be a paradigm shift from 'me' to 'her' or 'him.' One will stop doing things for himself/herself and start doing things for his/her spouse. It will be the beginning of destroying selfishness in oneself. We all agree that when selfishness no longer rules us, we go a long way in restoring the image of God, which was marred by sin in our lives.

It does not take two brilliant or good individuals who are married to reflect the image of God. It does not take a perfect, educated couple who are brought together by the institution of marriage to reflect the image of God. One does not need money or material things to achieve the goal of marriage. Actually, education, money and power can do a lot of harm to the quest of a couple to reflect the image of God. Rather, it requires two individuals who understand from the Bible's point of view why God brought them together. These two individuals (male and female) are imperfect sinners living in an imperfect, sinful world.

When a husband sees his imperfect wife shouting at him, he should pause and reflect, "In this situation, what should I do to this imperfect sinner that best represents how Christ would have dealt with the situation?" The reaction will not be to register how unhappy one is because of this treatment, but rather how best to mirror the image of Christ in the situation. The objective will no longer be that of retaliating but that of redemption. The words of Paul will begin to be applied in married life: "Husbands, love your wives, even as Christ also loved the church, and gave himself for it; That he might sanctify and cleanse it with the washing of water by the word, That he might present it to himself a glorious church, not having spot, or wrinkle, or any such thing; but that it should be holy and without blemish. So ought men to love their wives as their own bodies. For he that loveth his wife loveth himself. For no man ever yet hated his own flesh; but nourisheth and cherisheth it, even as the Lord of the church."

Did Christ love a perfect church? Did Christ die for the perfect church? The answer is no! By the same token, no man must expect to marry a perfect wife; otherwise, he will lose the opportunity to reflect on the character of Christ. The character of Christ is not reflected in a perfect situation but in an imperfect one. The character of Christ is not reflected in a holy situation but in a sinful one. If there had been no entrance of sin into the Garden of Eden, if Adam and Eve had remained in their perfect and sinless state as they were direct from the Creator's hands, there would have been no need for Christ. There would have been no need for a saviour.

This is the reason why God hates divorce. When a man divorces his wife, he fails to represent Christ in the home. He weighs all the weaknesses of his wife until he resolves that she is beyond redemption. There is no human being with such prerogatives. Christ Himself loved us, although we were still sinners. He died for the church, offered all for the church, and even today, He is interceding for the church. Before even considering divorcing his wife, a man must die for her first. He must literally die, for Christ literally died for the church.

There is another dimension to this mirror concept. We know that our characters are marred with sin, so we reflect sinful habits now and then. When a wife does something the husband perceives as wrong, the husband becomes angry and begins to curse her. In that instance, the wife acts as a mirror. She reflects this angry man who is far away from reflecting the image of God in the home. When a husband looks at himself in the mirror of his wife, his image is reflected. He understands his character. He might hide his true character from relatives, church members and the community, but he cannot hide his character from his wife. It is impossible for you to be a hypocrite in your own home. Therefore, the wife or the husband becomes an important mirror to reflect the character of his/her spouse. You can see and understand your character in your wife or husband. When you see how sinful your character is in the mirror of your spouse, you get back to your Saviour, renounce your sins, get back to your spouse, get angry, get back to Christ, be forgiven and get back to your spouse. When your spouse insults you, and you do not get angry, it means the marriage is achieving its purpose in your life.

The close intimacy between a husband and a wife allows them to reveal their weaknesses to each other. If the husband and the wife reveal their weaknesses to each other, they should not be desperate and angry, and the marriage will serve its purpose, which is to reveal sinful traits in a partner. When the partner discovers that, he or she must seek transformation from the Holy Spirit. God allows couples to stay together so that they can play a mirror role in each other's lives. The husband can see the reflection of his character in the mirror of his wife, while the wife can see the reflection of her character in the mirror of her husband. As the two continue to interact, they help each other to mould their characters in the similitude of Christ. As they mould their characters in the similitude of Christ, they become one in purpose and in mind.

The traits formed by married couples are the very traits that a Christian must develop to interact with any other person outside the marriage. We may call that person a neighbour. The Bible says to love our neighbour as ourselves. As the husband learns to love his wife as his own flesh, as he sacrifices himself for the sake of his wife, he might also learn to love his neighbour as himself and to sacrifice resources and time for the love of others. The marriage becomes a training school for righteousness, which must be manifested in the wider society before God takes us to the ultimate society of the righteous in heaven.

The training marriage offers for being holy should not be undermined. There is no other school that may offer such training. It is possible to live for a whole year without talking to your neighbour, even if there is something bothering you. You may say to yourself, "Let me leave this person alone; I don't want to be bothered. After all, I don't need anything from him. I have my own family, my own food, my own money." But it is not so with your spouse. You cannot avoid talking to a person whom you see every day. You cannot avoid talking to a person with whom you discuss the budget every day. You cannot avoid a person who is the mother or father of your children. You cannot avoid a person with whom everything in your life is intertwined. You cannot avoid a person with whom you have bought a house or a car, and most of all, you cannot avoid a person with whom you are now sharing a surname even though you were not born of the same parents.

As you seek to resolve issues with your spouse whom you cannot avoid, as you learn to be patient with your spouse, as you learn how to choose the words to speak to your spouse, as you learn how to resolve difficult matters for the sake of the person whom God has placed in your care; you conform to the likeness of Jesus. The character that the marriage will mould in you will become the character that the community will see in you, and the character that will ultimately take you to heaven. Those who perceive their marriages as impossible and their problems as irreconcilable fail to learn from the school of marriage. There is nothing irreconcilable in a marriage; it is only the attitudes of partners who do not know why God brought them together.

Those who fail to resolve their issues and decide to divorce forfeit their opportunities to mould their characters in the similitude of Christ and do not enter heaven. Normally, people who divorce their partners are the ones who are problematic. They are so full of self that they cannot compromise their standards to accommodate their spouse. They cannot submit to the other person. They cannot tolerate; they cannot love, for love "suffereth long, and is kind; love envieth not; love vaunteth not itself, is not puffed up; doth not behave itself unseemly, seeketh not her own, is not easily provoked, thinketh no evil; rejoiceth not in iniquity, but rejoiceth in the truth; beareth all things, believeth all things, hopeth all things, endureth all things. Love never faileth: but whether there be prophecies, they shall fail; whether there be tongues, they shall cease; whether there be knowledge, it shall vanish away" (1 Corinthians 13: 1-8). Love is a trait that can only be derived from the source, Jesus Christ. If you cannot love your spouse with heavenly love, how can you expect to love your neighbour as yourself? How can you expect to love your enemies and to pray for them? If any person fails in marriage, he dismally fails in this life and the life to come.

Remember Paul when he says, "Wherefore seeing we also are compassed about with so great a cloud of witnesses, let us lay aside every weight, and the sin which doth so easily beset us, and let us run with patience the race that is set before us, looking unto Jesus the author and finisher of our faith; who for the joy that was set before him endured the cross, despising the shame, and is set down at the right hand of the throne of God" (Hebrews 12: 1-3). Remember this, husband and wife. Your home is a little heaven where the husband is a representation of Christ Himself, and the wife is a representation of the church. The church must mirror the character of Jesus without spots or wrinkles, and Christ must mirror the church. When the characters of the two are merged into one, the union is consummated in the marriage supper of the lamb. All heaven and all the earth are a great cloud of witnesses that are cheering this marriage to soldier on until all is fulfilled when Christ shall marry His own.

12| The Image Restored

Matthew

25:1 – *Then shall the kingdom of heaven be likened unto ten virgins, which took their lamps, and went forth to meet the bridegroom.*

25:2 – *And five of them were wise, and five were foolish.*

25:3 – *They that were foolish took their lamps, and took no oil with them:*

25:4 – *But the wise took oil in their vessels with their lamps.*

25:5 – *While the bridegroom tarried, they all slumbered and slept.*

25:6 – *And at midnight there was a cry made, Behold, the bridegroom cometh; go ye out to meet him.*

25:7 – *Then all those virgins arose, and trimmed their lamps.*

25:8 – *And the foolish said unto the wise, "Give us of your oil; for our lamps are gone out."*

25:9 – *But the wise answered, saying, "Not so; lest there be not enough for us and you: but go ye rather to them that sell, and buy for yourselves."*

25:10 – *And while they went to buy, the bridegroom came; and they that were ready went in with him to the marriage: and the door was shut.*

Matthew

22:30 – *For in the resurrection they neither marry, nor are given in marriage, but are as the angels of God in heaven.*

Revelation

21:1 – *And I saw a new heaven and a new earth: for the first heaven and the first earth were passed away; and there was no more sea.*

21:2 – *And I John saw the holy city, new Jerusalem, coming down from God out of heaven, prepared as a bride adorned for her husband.*
21:3 – *And I heard a great voice out of heaven saying, "Behold, the tabernacle of God is with men, and he will dwell with them, and they shall be his people, and God himself shall be with them, and be their God.*
21:4 – *And God shall wipe away all tears from their eyes; and there shall be no more death, neither sorrow, nor crying, neither shall there be any more pain: for the former things are passed away."*
Revelation
19:7 – *Let us be glad and rejoice, and give honour to him: for the marriage of the Lamb is come, and his wife hath made herself ready.*
19:8 – *And to her was granted that she should be arrayed in fine linen, clean and white: for the fine linen is the righteousness of saints.*
19:9 – *And he saith unto me, "Write, Blessed are they which are called unto the marriage supper of the Lamb." And he saith unto me, "These are the true sayings of God."*
19:10 – *And I fell at his feet to worship him. And he said unto me, "See thou do it not: I am thy fellow servant, and of thy brethren that have the testimony of Jesus: worship God: for the testimony of Jesus is the spirit of prophecy."*

As we conclude our discourse on marriage, let me once again remind you of the purpose for which God originated and ordained marriage. When God created Adam and Eve and commanded them to be faithful and multiply, He wanted them to replenish the earth with sinless human beings, but they were placed on probation. If Adam and Eve had passed the probation, they would have been elevated to the positions that were left vacant by the devil and his evil angels. Adam was supposed to occupy the position left by

Lucifer himself. But that was before sin entered the planet Earth. After Adam and Eve were deceived by the devil, and the marriage was marred by sin, God did not change His purpose for marriage. God could not change His purpose because of the slight setback caused by the intrusion of sin. When sin entered the planet Earth, God allowed the plan of redemption to be rolled on. The plan of redemption had been prepared before the foundations of the earth. Instead of the human family dying, Jesus offered to take their place so that the purposes of God for marriage might still continue. The human family has been placed on probation again: if they have faith in the merits of Jesus, they can be made holy again, and the image of God that was marred by sin can be restored again. Through the blood of Jesus, when the image of God is fully restored again, man will be elevated to the position of an angel, and heaven will become his home. The purpose that people who are in a union called marriage should seek to achieve is: the restoration of the image of God in humanity.

As we are in our marriage, we should not forget that we are living in a probationary period. We are living in a period of waiting. We are waiting for the second coming of Jesus, for Him to take us to heaven to be in the company of angels. But our characters need to be holy before that happens. Therefore, Christ is also waiting. He is waiting for our marriages to train us into holiness through His merits. Through his blood that was shed on the cross of Calvary, Jesus Christ promised us to overcome sin. But Christ cannot wait for us forever. After a certain time, He will decide that enough is enough and will come to fetch only those who will comply with this plan of salvation. That's why our marriages are likened unto ten virgins. Five were foolish, and five were clever. Each marriage will fit in either of the two categories. The clever ones will develop their characters so that when Christ comes, they will be prepared to meet Him.

It might seem that the bridegroom is no longer coming, but the Bible says eventually, he did come. When he arrived, there were some who were relaxing, and they failed to keep enough oil in their lamps. But the wise remained vigilant. Their lamps had enough oil to meet the bridegroom. When the bridegroom arrived, those who had developed righteous characters during their period of waiting went inside the house for the marriage, and the door was shut. It, therefore, follows that our marriages now are preparing us for the big marriage in heaven, the marriage of Christ and His church.

If we keep in mind that we are on probation and the bridegroom will definitely come one day, our preparation here should be thorough. Nothing should be left to chance. Our marriages should thoroughly work righteousness in us, for the final consummation of the earthly marriage will be realised in the heavenly marriage.

There are people who do not want to enjoy God's gift of marriage now and all the benefits associated with it – the joy of sharing, edification, sex and procreation, to mention a few. They think they will marry in the world to come, but the marriage that will be in heaven is the union of Christ (husband) and His church (the wife). Jesus, in His words, alluded to the fact that the redeemed of the earth will be like angels in heaven, where they do not marry.

In the probation period, the couple should take advantage of the lessons they learn in this sacred union and impart the same to their children, who will eventually get married as well. When their children get married, they will do likewise. When we are cleansed by the blood of the lamb through our marriages and the family, we become partakers of Christ's righteousness. We become clothed with the white linen, which is Christ's righteousness. Blessed and holy are the ones who will have such a preparation, for they will be invited to the wedding supper of the lamb. All marriages across the planet, where the individuals manage to develop in a way that reproduces the character of Jesus in his/her life, will make up the multitudes who will stand before the Saviour. There will be no more death, suffering, divorces, or diseases; behold, everything will be made new. All the marriages will be fulfilled in one big marriage in heaven. The righteousness of saints is by marriage, through the blood of the lamb.

Revelation 19:9 – And he saith unto me, "Write, blessed are they which are called unto the marriage supper of the lamb." And he saith unto me, "These are the true sayings of God."

Jude 1:24 – Now unto him that is able to keep you from falling, and to present you faultless before the presence of his glory with exceeding joy, to the only wise God our saviour, be glory and majesty, dominion and power, both now and for ever.
Amen.

www.ingramcontent.com/pod-product-compliance
Lightning Source LLC
Chambersburg PA
CBHW050021170726
48282CB00025B/492
9788119524488